FARNSWORTH'S CHARGE.

THREE DAYS AT GETTYSBURG: July 1, 2 & 3, 1863
by General Henry J. Hunt
FOREWORD

The Confederate Army under General Lee was on its way north. Washington, D.C., seemed within striking distance, with the Southern Army strong in terms both of morale — after their victories in the battles of Fredericksburg and Chancellorsville — and also in terms of equipment and experience. The Northern Army, under a changing succession of leaders and still looking for their first major victory, thought the South might succeed, and prepared for the defense.

Of course, the South was repulsed. But it is hard to say who won, for both sides lost heavily and about equally. Modern estimates place the number of soldiers killed, wounded, or missing in this one clash at 51,000!

Our account comes from no latter-day historian's efforts to refabricate the action. Author General Hunt was there, directing the artillery for the North's Army of the Potomac. He did, however, have the advantage of a historian's later perspective, for publication did not occur for over two decades after the battle. The material was first printed in 1886-87 by *Century Magazine,* a national journal of that early day with a circulation to a million readers. Most of the illustrations here accompanied the original article; a few have been added from other Century Civil War articles of the same period.

Military historians and Civil War buffs will find this detailed account of value and a good almost blow-by-blow record of the three days' battles; all will find that it helps place in perspective the importance of the Gettysburg defense in preserving the United States of America, then not even a century old.

William R. Jones
Series Editor

Copyright © 1981 OUTBOOKS, 217 Kimball Avenue, Golden, Colorado 80401

ISBN 0-89646-036-3

CHARGE OF ALEXANDER'S ARTILLERY.

HISTORIAN'S PREFACE

This account of the three days of conflict in and around the town of Gettysburg, Pennsylvania in July 1863 was written by the commander of Federal artillery during that summer's campaign. Henry Hunt submitted this three-part series of articles to the New York-based *Century Magazine* in 1886-1887, and was pleased to see it included in that company's publication *Battles and Leaders of the Civil War*. This series of articles became the basic narrative in *Battles and Leaders* for an impartial and authoritative early account of the Battle of Gettysburg.

Hunt, as chief of artillery in the Union Army of the Potomac, did not neglect the role of that branch of the service, as most authors before and after him have done. Instead, the preponderance of his narrative deals with both Union and Confederate batteries, with the infantry and cavalry actions as a backdrop. Still the history recounted by Hunt is general and concise enough to be understood by the layman and the new student of the battle.

Fault can be found in the narrative, however, over minor points such as numerical or battery strengths, nomenclature, oversight, and some amount of bias, which cannot be ignored by the more serious students of the battle. Where such gross errors or biases appear, they are corrected or commented upon in the numbered footnotes found in the back. Many of the illustrations which appeared in the *Century* editions were mislabeled and are so noted and explained via the footnotes.

Any student of the battle who reads the narrative will notice the striking difference between Henry Hunt's history and that written by Major-General Abner Doubleday (*Chancellorsville and Gettysburg,* Campaigns of the Civil War, vol. VI New York, 1882). Both officers were unjustly ignored by superiors and early historians for their respective roles in the battle, and both were sensitive to this abuse by silence. Doubleday was obviously distrusted so much by General George Meade (then commanding the Army of the Potomac) that after the death of Major John F. Reynolds he was replaced as First Corps Commander by an officer from an entirely different corps. Reynolds was technically First Corps Commander, but was also given command of the entire army's "left wing" during this phase of the campaign (which would have given him authority over the Eleventh Corps as well as his own on the opening day of the battle). While Reynolds enjoyed this overall command, Doubleday had headed the First Corps. Still smarting from the injustice of having his corps command taken from him after he and his men had performed so valiantly on July 1, Doubleday used his history of the battle to extoll that valor and to condemn that of other corps. Hunt, on the other hand, was preeminently trusted by Meade and his battery commanders. Unfortunately, his unassuming character and his "wrong" politics did little to further his career, and he would die long after the war with only a colonel's commission.

Hunt was highly respected by his fellow artillerymen; he was tenacious and resourceful in battle and was not one to make excuses or sling mud when things went badly for him. At Gettysburg, Hunt had semi-independent command and was more active than his commander-in-chief Meade in visiting all parts of the battlefield (when Hunt was present, that is, from the night of July 1 to July 3). Because the Union Army of the Potomac had the interior line, Hunt was enabled to effectively juggle his available field guns from one threatened site to another, and, at times, found his guns holding parts of this line alone against attacking Southerners without the support of infantry.

Although General Hunt does not give as complete or accurate an account of Confederate artillery or infantry movements, his history is fairer to his old enemy than most of his compatriots' reminiscences, and attempts to give the reader an uncluttered overview of the events of that fateful campaign. In this way Hunt was eminently more successful than Doubleday and many later historians. His history is still readable and informative, and may be the best introductory history of this great Civil War battle.

Research Historian
National Park Service
Gettysburg National Military Park

BUFORD'S CAVALRY OPPOSING THE CONFEDERATE ADVANCE UPON GETTYSBURG.

THE BATTLE OF THE FIRST DAY AT GETTYSBURG.

THE battles of Fredericksburg and Chancellorsville raised the confidence of the Confederate army of Northern Virginia to such a height as to cause its subordinate officers and soldiers to believe that, as opposed to the Army of the Potomac, they were equal to any demand that could be made upon them. Their belief in the superiority of the Southerner to the Northerner as a fighter was no longer, as at the beginning of the war, a mere provincial conceit, for it was now supported by signal successes in the field. On each of these two occasions the Army of the Potomac had been recently reorganized under a new general, presumably abler than his predecessor and possessing the confidence of the War Department, and the results were crowning victories for the Confederates. Yet at Fredericksburg defeat was not owing to any lack of fighting qualities on the part of the Federal soldier, but rather to defective leadership.

At Chancellorsville both qualities were called in question. In none of the previous battles between these armies had the disparity of numbers been so great. The Federal general had taken the initiative, his plan of operations was excellent, and his troops eager for battle. The Confederates could at first oppose but a portion of their inferior force to the attack of greatly superior numbers, and the boast of the Federal commander, that "the Army of Northern Virginia was the legitimate property of the Army of the Potomac," seemed in a fair way to be justified, when at the first contact the advantages already gained were thrown away, and a timid defensive attitude assumed. Lee's bold offensive which followed immediately on this exhibition of weakness, the consequent rout of a Federal army-corps, and the subsequent retreat of the whole army, a large portion of which had not been engaged, confirmed the exultant Confederates in their conviction — which now became an article of faith — that both in combat and in generalship the superiority of the Southerner was fully established. The Federal soldiers returned to their camps on the northern bank of the Rappahannock, mortified and incensed at finding themselves, through no fault of their own, in the condition of having in an offensive campaign lost a battle without fighting, except when the enemy forced it upon them.

Yet in this battle the Northern soldier fought well. No men could under the circumstances have withstood such a sudden attack as that made by "Stonewall" Jackson on the flank and rear of the Eleventh Corps; but as soon as Jackson encountered troops in condition for action, his pursuit was checked and he was brought to a stand. The panic did not extend beyond the routed corps, nor to all of that, for its artillery and so much of its infantry as could form a proper line did their duty, and the army, far from being " demoralized " by this mishap, simply ridiculed the corps which from its supposed want of vigilance had allowed itself to be surprised in a position in which it could not fight. The surprise itself was not the fault of the troops, and the corps redeemed its reputation in subsequent battles. Both armies were composed in the main of Americans, and there was little more difference between their men than might be found between those of either army at different periods, or under varying circumstances; for although high bounties had already brought into the Federal ranks an inferior element which swelled the muster rolls and the number of stragglers, "bounty jumping" had not as yet become a regular business.

The morale of the Confederate army was, however, much higher at this time than that of its adversary. It was composed of men not less patriotic, many of whom had gone into the war with reluctance, but who now felt that they were defending their homes. They were by this time nearly all veterans, led by officers having the confidence of their government, which took pains to inspire its soldiers with the same feeling. Their successes were extolled and magnified; their reverses palliated or ignored. Exaggerations as to the relative numbers of the troops had been common enough on both sides, but those indulged in at the South had been echoed, sometimes suggested, in the North by a portion of the press and people, so that friends and enemies united in inspiring in the Confederate soldier a belief in himself and a contempt for his enemy.

In the Army of the Potomac it was different; the proportion of veterans was much smaller; a cessation of recruiting at the very beginning of active operations, when men were easily obtainable to supply losses in existing regiments, had been followed, as emergencies arose, by new levies for short periods of service, and in new organizations which could not readily be assimilated by older troops. And there were special difficulties. The Army of the Potomac was not in favor at the War Department. Rarely, if ever, had it heard a word of official commendation after a success, or of sympathy or encouragement after a defeat. From the very beginning its camps had been filled with imputations and charges against its leaders, who were accused on the streets, by the press, in Congress, and even in the War Department itself, and after victories as well as after defeats, not only of incapacity or misconduct, but sometimes of "disloyalty" to their superiors, civil and military, and even to the cause for which they fought. These accusations were followed or accompanied by frequent changes of commanders of the army, army-corps, and even of divisions. Under such circumstances, but little confidence could be felt by the troops, either in the wisdom of a war office which seemed to change its favorites with the caprice of a coquette, or in the capacity of new generals who followed each other in such rapid succession. But it is due to that patient and sorely tried army, to say that the spirit of both its officers and men was of the best, and their devotion to

THE LUTHERAN SEMINARY. (THE UPPER PICTURE FROM A WAR-TIME PHOTOGRAPH.)
Both pictures show the seminary as facing the town, and in the right-hand view is seen the Chambersburg Pike. On the first day, Buford, Reynolds, and Howard used the cupola for observations; thereafter it was the chief signal-station and observatory for the Confederates.—EDITOR.*

duty unconquerable. The army itself had originally been so admirably disciplined and tempered, that there always remained to it a firm self-reliance and a stern sense of duty and of honor that was proof against its many discouragements. In battle it always acquitted itself well, and displayed the highest soldierly qualities, no matter who commanded it nor whence he came. Chancellorsville furnishes no exception to this assertion, nor evidence of inferiority of the Northern to the Southern soldier, but it does furnish striking illustrations of Napoleon's well-known saying, "In war men are nothing, *a man* is everything."

*Notes in text signed thus are by the original *Century Magazine* editor.

THE BATTLE OF THE FIRST DAY AT GETTYSBURG.

GENERAL LEE'S HEADQUARTERS ON THE CHAMBERSBURG PIKE. (FROM A WAR-TIME PHOTOGRAPH.)

This dwelling, which stands on the Chambersburg Pike where it crosses Seminary ridge, is called Lee's headquarters; the tents of the Confederate general were pitched in the yard behind the house. Editor.

General Lee, who felt great confidence in his own troops, and overrated the effects of successive reverses on the Federal soldiers, now resolved to assume the offensive, for he knew that to remain on the defensive would in the end force him back on Richmond. He determined, therefore, in case the Army of the Potomac could not be brought to action under favorable circumstances in Virginia, to transfer, if permitted, the field of operations to Northern soil, where a victory promptly followed up would give him possession of Baltimore or Washington, and perhaps lead to the recognition of the Confederacy by foreign powers. The valley of the Shenandoah offered a safe line of operations; the Federal troops occupying it were rather a bait than an obstacle, and to capture or destroy them seemed quite practicable to one who controlled absolutely all Confederate troops within the sphere of his operations. The sharp lesson he had administered the previous year had not been heeded by the Federal War Office; an opportunity now offered to repeat it, and he took his measures accordingly. In case his government would not consent to a bolder offensive, he could at least clear the valley of Virginia of the enemy,— a distinct operation, yet a necessary preliminary to an invasion of the North. This work was assigned to Lieutenant-General Ewell, an able officer, in every way qualified for such an enterprise.

In anticipation of the new campaign, Lee's army was strengthened and reorganized into three army corps* of three divisions each. Each division consisted of four brigades, except Rodes's and Anderson's, which had five each, and Pickett's, which had three at Gettysburg,— in all, thirty-seven infantry brigades. The cavalry were the select troops of the Confederacy. Officers and men had been accustomed all their lives to the use of horses and arms, "and to the very end the best blood in the land rode after Stuart, Hampton, and the Lees." They were now organized as a division, under Major-General J. E. B. Stuart, consisting of the six brigades of Hampton, Robertson, Fitzhugh Lee, Jenkins, Jones, and W. H. F. Lee, and six batteries of horse-artillery under Major R. F. Beckham. To these should be added Imboden's command, a strong brigade of over two thousand effective horsemen, and a battery of horse-artillery, which had been operating in the mountain country and was now near Staunton, awaiting orders. The

---

* First Corps, Longstreet: divisions, McLaws, Pickett, Hood; artillery, Walton.
Second Corps, Ewell: divisions, Early, Johnson, Rodes; artillery, Brown.
Third Corps, A. P. Hill: divisions, R. H. Anderson, Heth, Pender; artillery, Walker.— H. J. H.

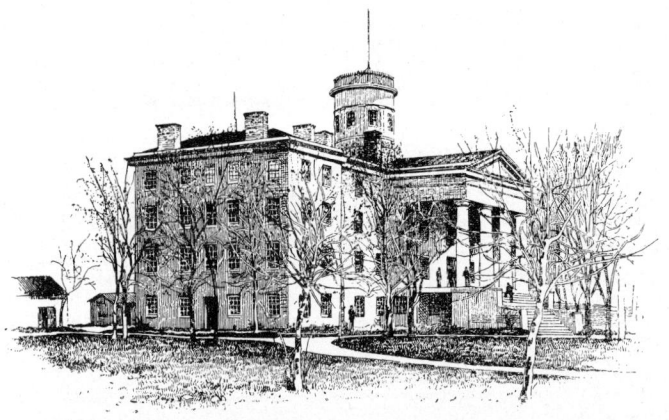

PENNSYLVANIA COLLEGE, GETTYSBURG. (FROM A PHOTOGRAPH BY TIPTON.)

During the withdrawal of the First and Eleventh Corps through the town to Cemetery Hill, there was hard fighting in the college grounds.— EDITOR.

artillery had recently received an excellent organization under its commandant-in-chief, General Pendleton. It consisted, besides the horse-artillery, of fifteen so-called "battalions," each of four batteries, with one lieutenant-colonel and a major.[2] To each army-corps were attached five battalions, one for each division and two as a reserve, the whole under a colonel as chief of artillery. The total number of batteries was sixty-nine, of guns two hundred and eighty-seven, of which thirty were with the cavalry. With few exceptions the batteries were of four guns each. The army was commanded by a full general, each army-corps, except the artillery, by a lieutenant-generals and twenty-nine colonels. The average strength of army corps and divisions was about half that of the Confederates, a fact that should be kept in mind, or the terms will be misleading. The cavalry had been raised under disadvantages. Men accustomed to the use of both horses and arms were comparatively few in the North and required training in everything that was necessary to make a trooper. The theater of war was not considered favorable for cavalry, and it was distributed to the various headquarters for escort duty, guards, and orderlies. It was not until 1863 that it was united under General Pleasonton in a corps consisting of three weak

GETTYSBURG FROM OAK HILL. (FROM A PHOTOGRAPH BY TIPTON.)

Oak Hill is a mile north-west of Gettysburg, and the view here is south-east, showing the county almshouse on the left, then Culp's Hill, then the college, and, to the right of its cupola, the observatory on Cemetery Hill.— EDITOR.

ant-general, each division by a major-general, each brigade, except two, by brigadier-generals. Nearly all these officers were veterans of proved ability and many had served in the Mexican war.

In the Army of the Potomac the discharge of fifty-eight regiments had reduced its strength since Chancellorsville by twenty-five thousand effectives, partly replaced by five brigades numbering less than twelve thousand men. At the battle of Gettysburg the seven army-corps[*] consisted of nineteen infantry divisions, seven of which had two brigades, eleven had three, and one had four: in all fifty-one brigades. The army and army-corps were commanded by major-generals, the divisions by three major- and sixteen brigadier-generals, the infantry brigades by twenty-two brigadier-divisions, Buford's, D. McM. Gregg's, and Duffié's, afterwards consolidated into two, Stahel's cavalry, which joined at Frederick, June 28th, becoming the third division. The corps was then organized as follows: First Division, Buford: brigades, Gamble, Devin, Merritt; Second Division, Gregg: brigades, McIntosh, Huey, J. Irvin Gregg; Third Division, Kilpatrick: brigades, Farnsworth, Custer. The divisions and three of the brigades were commanded by brigadier-generals, the other five brigades by colonels. To the cavalry were attached Robertson's and Tidball's brigades of horse-artillery. Under excellent chiefs and the spirit created by its new organization, the Federal cavalry soon rivaled that of the Confederates.

The field-artillery was in an unsatisfactory

---

[*] First Corps, J. F. Reynolds: divisions, Wadsworth, Robinson, Doubleday; artillery, Wainwright. Second Corps, Hancock: divisions, Caldwell, Gibbon, Alexander Hays; artillery, Hazard. Third Corps, Sickles: divisions, Birney, Humphreys; artillery, Randolph. Fifth Corps, Sykes: divisions, Barnes, Ayres, Crawford; artillery, A. P. Martin. Sixth Corps, Sedgwick: divisions, Wright, Howe, Wheaton; artillery, Tompkins. Eleventh Corps, Howard: divisions, Barlow, Steinwehr, Schurz; artillery, Osborn. Twelfth Corps,
Slocum: divisions, A. S. Williams, Geary; artillery, Muhlenberg.
Engineers, commandant-in-chief, G. K. Warren; Engineer brigade, Benham.
Artillery, commandant-in-chief, Hunt; artillery reserve, Tyler: brigades of Ransom, McGilvery, Taft, Huntington, Fitzhugh.
General Headquarters, Chief of Staff Butterfield, Adjutant-General Williams, Inspector-General Schriver, Provost-Marshal General Patrick.— H. J. H.

MAJOR-GENERAL JOHN F. REYNOLDS.

(FROM A PHOTOGRAPH BY BRADY.)

condition. The high reputation it had gained in Mexico was followed by the active and persistent hostility of the War Department, which almost immediately dismounted three-fourths of its authorized batteries. Congress in 1853 made special provision for remounting them as schools of instruction for the whole arm, a duty which the War Department on shallow pretexts evaded. Again in 1861, Congress amply provided for the proper organization and command of the artillery in the field, but as there was no chief nor special administration for the arm, and no regulations for its government, its organization control and direction were left to the fancies of the various army commanders. General officers were practically denied it, and in 1862 the War Department announced in orders that field-officers of artillery were an unnecessary expense and their muster into service forbidden. Promotion necessarily ceased, and such brilliant artillerists as Hays, DeRussy, Getty, Gibbon, Griffin, and Ayres could only receive promotion by transfer to the infantry or cavalry. No adequate measures were taken for the supply of recruits, and the batteries were frequently dependent on the troops to which they were attached for men enough to work their guns in battle. For battery-draft they were often glad to get the refuse horses after the ambulance and quartermasters' trains were supplied. Still, many of the batteries attained a high degree of excellence, due mainly to the self-sacrifice, courage, and intelligence of their own officers and men.[3]

On taking command of the army, General Hooker had transferred the military command of the artillery to his own headquarters, to be resumed by the chief of artillery only under specific orders and for special occasions, which resulted in such mismanagement and confusion at Chancellorsville that he consented to organize the artillery into brigades. This was a decided improvement, which would have been greater if the brigade commanders had held adequate rank. As it was, there was no artillery commandant-in-chief for months before the battle of Gettysburg, and of the fourteen brigades four were commanded by field-officers, nine by captains, and one by a lieutenant, taken from their batteries for the purpose. The number of field batteries at Gettysburg was sixty-five, of guns three hundred and seventy, of which two hundred and twelve were with the infantry, fifty with the cavalry, one hundred and eight in the reserve.[4] The disadvantages under which the artillery labored all through the war, from want of proper regulations, supervision, and command, were simply disgraceful to our army administration from the close of the Mexican to that of the Civil War, and caused an unnecessary expenditure of both blood and treasure.

It will be perceived by comparison that the organization of the Army of the Potomac was at this period in every way inferior to that of its adversary. The army-corps and divisions were too numerous and too weak. They required too many commanders and staffs, and this imposed unnecessary burdens on the general-in-chief, who was often compelled to

NORTH-EAST CORNER OF THE McPHERSON WOODS, WHERE GENERAL REYNOLDS WAS KILLED.
(FROM A PHOTOGRAPH BY TIPTON.)

The McPherson Farm buildings, on the Chambersburg Pike, are seen in the background. Reynolds's first line of artillery lay across the pike near these buildings.— EDITOR.

place several army-corps under the commander of one of them, thus reproducing the much abused "grand divisions" of Burnside, under every possible disadvantage. Had the number of infantry corps been reduced to four at most, and the divisions to twelve, the army would have been more manageable and better commanded, and the artillery, without any loss, but rather a gain of efficiency, could have been reduced by a dozen or fifteen batteries.

EARLY in June Lee's army began to move, and by the 8th, Longstreet's and Ewell's corps had joined Stuart's cavalry at Culpeper. A. P. Hill's corps was left in observation at Fredericksburg; and so skillfully were the changes concealed that Hooker, believing that all the enemy's infantry were still near that town, ordered Pleasonton to beat up Stuart's camps at Culpeper, and get information as to the enemy's position and proposed movements. For these purposes he gave

Pleasonton two small brigades of infantry, 3000 men under Generals Ames and Russell, which carried his total force to 10,981. They were echeloned along the railroad which crosses the river at Rappahannock Station, and runs thence ten miles to Culpeper. About midway is Brandy Station, a few hundred yards north of which is Fleetwood Hill. Dividing his force equally, Pleasonton ordered Buford and Ames to cross at Beverly's, and

LUTHERAN CHURCH ON CHAMBERSBURG STREET, USED AS A HOSPITAL. (FROM A PHOTOGRAPH BY TIPTON.)

Gregg, Duffié, and Russell at Kelly's Ford. All were to march to Brandy Station, Duffié being thrown out to Stevensburg to watch the Fredericksburg road. Then the whole force was to move on Culpeper. The crossing was ordered for June 9th; but on the 8th, General Lee having sent Jenkins's brigade as Ewell's advance into the valley, reviewed the other five brigades of Stuart, 10,292 combatants, on the plains near Brandy Station. After the review they were distributed in the neighborhood with a view to their crossing the Rappahannock on the 9th, Stuart establishing his headquarters at Fleetwood. Accident had thus disposed his forces in the most favorable manner to meet Pleasonton's converging movements.

At daybreak Buford crossed and drove the enemy's pickets from the ford back to the main body, near St. James's church. Stuart, on the first report of the crossing, sent Robertson's brigade toward Kelly's to watch that ford, and Colonel M. C. Butler's Second South Carolina to Brandy Station. He himself took the command at the church where he was attacked by Buford. In one of the engagements W. H. F. Lee was wounded, and Colonel Chambliss took command of his brigade. Meantime Gregg had crossed at Kelly's Ford, and, Duffié leading, took a southerly road, by which he missed Robertson's brigade. Learning that Duffié's advance had reached Stevensburg and that Buford was heavily engaged, Gregg pushed direct for Brandy Station, sending orders to Duffié to follow his movement. Stuart, notified of his approach, had sent in haste some artillery and two of Jones's regiments to Fleetwood, and Colonel Butler started at once for Stevensburg, followed soon after by Wickham's Fourth Virginia. On their approach two squadrons of the Sixth Ohio, in occupation of the place, fell back skirmishing. Duffié sent two regiments to their aid, and after a severe action, mainly with the Second South Carolina, reoccupied the village. In this action Colonel Butler lost a leg, and his lieutenant-colonel, Hampton, was killed.

On Gregg's arrival near Brandy Station the enemy appeared to be in large force, with artillery, on and about Fleetwood Hill. He promptly ordered an attack; the hill was carried, and the two regiments sent by Stuart driven back. Buford now attacked vigorously and gained ground steadily, for Stuart had to reënforce his troops at Fleetwood from the church. In the struggles that followed, the hill several times changed masters; but as Duffié did not make his appearance, Gregg was finally overmatched and withdrew, leaving three of his guns, two of them disabled, in the enemy's hands, nearly all of their horses being killed and most of their cannoneers *hors de combat*. There were some demonstrations of pursuit, but the approach of Buford's reserve brigade stopped them. Duffié finally came up and Gregg reported to Pleasonton, informing him of the approach of Confederate infantry from Culpeper. Pleasonton, who had captured some important dispatches and orders, now considered his mission as accomplished, and ordered a withdrawal of his whole command. This was effected leisurely and without molestation. Gregg recrossed at Rappahannock Station, Buford at Beverly's Ford, and at sunset the river again flowed between the opposing forces. Stuart reports his losses at four hundred and eighty-five, of whom three hundred and one were killed or wounded. Pleasonton reports an aggregate loss (exclusive of Duffié's, which would not exceed twenty-five) of nine hundred and seven, of whom

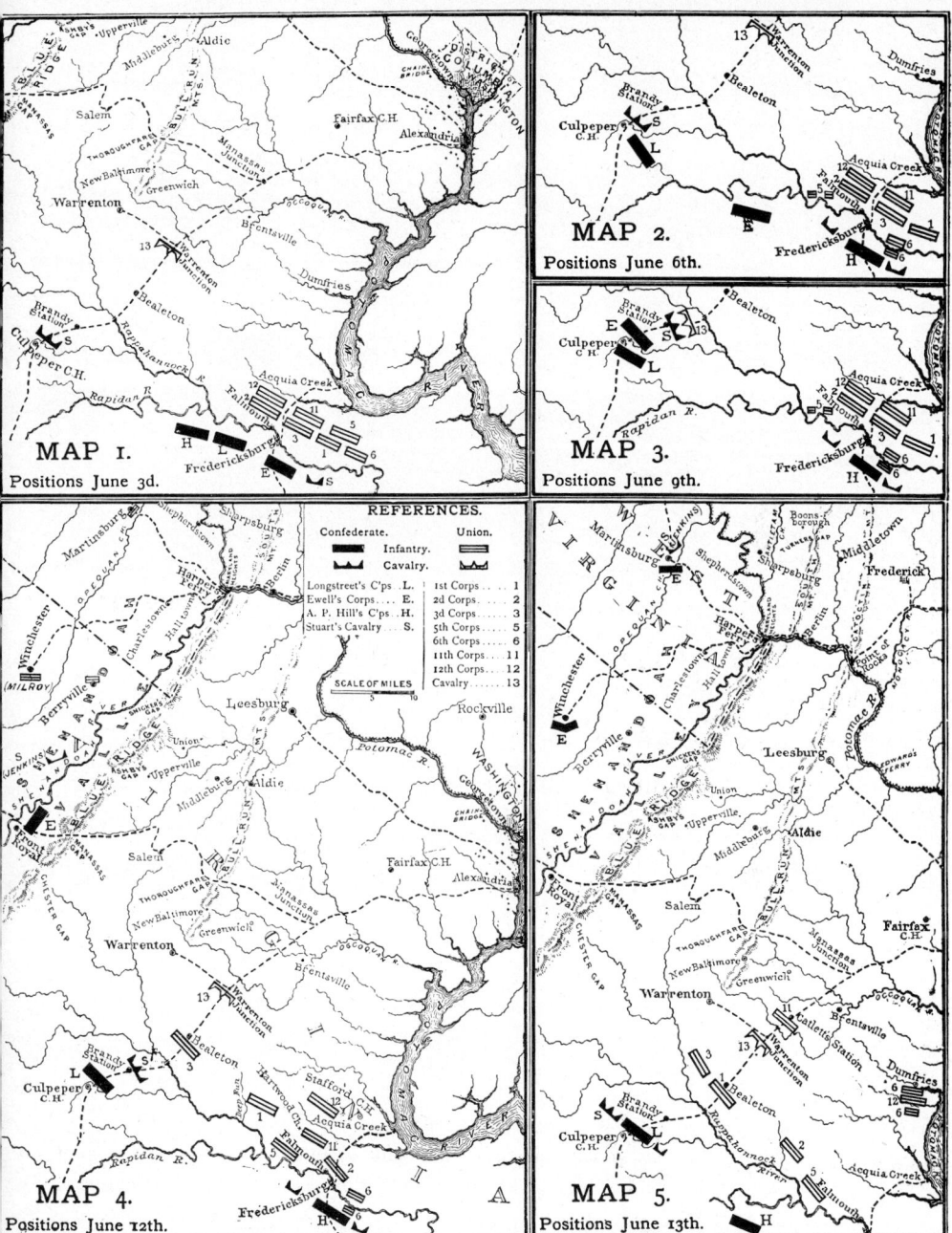

These maps and the others relating to the campaign and battle of Gettysburg are compilations by Abner Doubleday, Brevet Major-General, U. S. A., from the official reports of the commanders on both sides, and from the maps of Colonel John B. Bachelder, which were purchased by Congress for the War Department.— EDITOR.

four hundred and twenty-one were killed or wounded. In nearly all the previous so-called "cavalry" actions, the troops had fought as dismounted dragoons. This was in the main a true cavalry battle, and enabled the Federals henceforth to dispute the superiority hitherto claimed by, and conceded to, the Confederate cavalry. In this respect the affair was an important one. It did not, however, delay for a moment General Lee's designs on the valley; he had already sent Imboden by way of Romney toward Cumberland to destroy the railroad and canal from that place to Martinsburg.

UNION DEAD WEST OF THE SEMINARY. (FROM A PHOTOGRAPH.) 5

Milroy's Federal division, about nine thousand strong, occupied Winchester, with McReynolds's brigade in observation at Berryville. Kelley's division of about ten thousand men was at Harper's Ferry, with a detachment of twelve hundred infantry and a battery under Colonel B. F. Smith at Martinsburg. On the night of June 11th, Milroy received instructions to join Kelley, but, reporting that he could hold Winchester, was authorized to remain there. Ewell, leaving Brandy Station June 10, reached Cedarville via Chester Gap on the evening of the 12th, whence he detached Jenkins and Rodes to capture McReynolds, who, discovering their approach, withdrew to Winchester. They then pushed on to Martinsburg, and on the 14th drove out the garrison. Smith's infantry crossed the Potomac at Shepherdstown, and made its way to Maryland Heights; his artillery retreated by the Williamsport road, was pursued, and lost five guns.

Meanwhile Ewell, with Early's and Edward Johnson's divisions, marched direct on Winchester. Arriving in its neighborhood on the evening of the 13th, he ordered Early on the 14th to leave a brigade in observation on the south of the town, move his main force under cover of the hills to the north-western side, and seize the outworks which commanded the main fort. He also ordered Johnson to deploy his division on the east of the town, so as to divert attention from Early. This was so successfully done that the latter placed, unperceived, twenty guns and an assaulting column in position, and at 6 P. M., by a sudden attack, carried the outworks, driving the garrisons into the body of the place. This capture was a complete surprise, and Milroy called a council of war, which decided on an immediate retreat, abandoning the artillery and wagons. Ewell had anticipated this, and ordered Johnson to occupy with a brigade a position on the Martinsburg pike, north of Winchester. The retreat commenced at two A. M. of the 15th, and after proceeding three or four miles, the advance encountered Johnson's troops, attacked vigorously, and at first successfully, but the enemy receiving reënforcements, a hard fight ensued in which the Federals lost heavily. The retreat was then continued; the troops separated in the darkness, one portion reaching Harper's Ferry, another crossing the Potomac at Hancock. On the 15th, Ewell crossed the river, occupied Hagerstown and Sharpsburg, and sent Jenkins's cavalry to Chambersburg to collect supplies. On the 17th, the garrison of Harper's Ferry was removed to Maryland Heights, and the valley of the Shenandoah was cleared of Federal troops. In these brilliant operations General Lee claims for Ewell the capture of four thousand prisoners and small arms, twenty-eight pieces of artillery, eleven colors, three hundred loaded wagons, as many horses, and a considerable quantity of stores of all descriptions, the entire Confederate loss, killed, wounded, and missing, being two hundred and sixty-nine.

These operations indicate on the part of General Lee either contempt for his opponent, or a belief that the chronic terror of the War Department for the safety of Washington could be safely relied upon to paralyze his movements,— or both. On no other reasonable hypothesis can we account for his stretching his army from Fredericksburg to Williamsport, with his enemy concentrated on one flank, and on the shortest road to Richmond.

General Hooker's instructions were to keep always in view the safety of Washington and Harper's Ferry, and this necessarily subordinated his operations to those of the enemy. On June 5th, he reported that in case Lee moved via Culpeper toward the Potomac with his main body, leaving a corps at Fredericksburg, he should consider it his duty to attack the latter, and asked if that would be within the spirit of his instructions. In reply he was warned against such a course, and its dangers to Washington and Harper's Ferry were pointed out. On June 10th, learning that Lee was in motion, and that there were but few troops in Richmond, he proposed an immediate march on that place, from which, after capturing it, he could send the disposable part of his force to any threatened point north of the Potomac, and was informed that Lee's army and not Richmond was his true objective. Had he taken Richmond, Peck's large force at Suffolk and Keyes's ten thousand men in the Peninsula might have been utilized, and Hooker's whole army set free for operations against Lee.

As yet an invasion of the North had not been definitely fixed upon. On June 8th, the day before Brandy Station, General Lee, in a confidential letter to Mr. Seddon, Confederate Secretary of War, stated that he was aware of the hazard of taking the aggressive, yet nothing was to be gained by remaining on the defensive; still, if the department thought it better to do so, he would adopt that course. Mr. Seddon replied June 10th, the date of Hooker's proposal to march on Richmond, concurring in General Lee's views. He considered aggressive action indispensable, that "all attendant risks and sacrifices must be incurred," and adds, "I have not hesitated in coöperating with your plans to leave this city almost defenseless." General Lee now had full liberty of action, with the assured support of his government,— an immense advantage over an opponent who had neither.

So soon as Hooker learned from Pleasonton that a large infantry force was at Culpeper, he extended his right up the Rappahannock, and when informed of Ewell's move toward the valley, being forbidden to attack A. P. Hill at Fredericksburg or to spoil Lee's plans by marching to Richmond, he moved his army, on the night of June 13th, toward the line of the Orange and Alexandria Railroad, and occupied Thoroughfare Gap in advance of it. On the 15th, Longstreet left Culpeper, keeping east of the Blue Ridge and so covering its gaps. On the 14th, Hill left Fredericksburg, and via Chester Gap reached Shepherds-

UNION DEAD NEAR McPHERSON'S WOODS. (FROM A PHOTOGRAPH.)

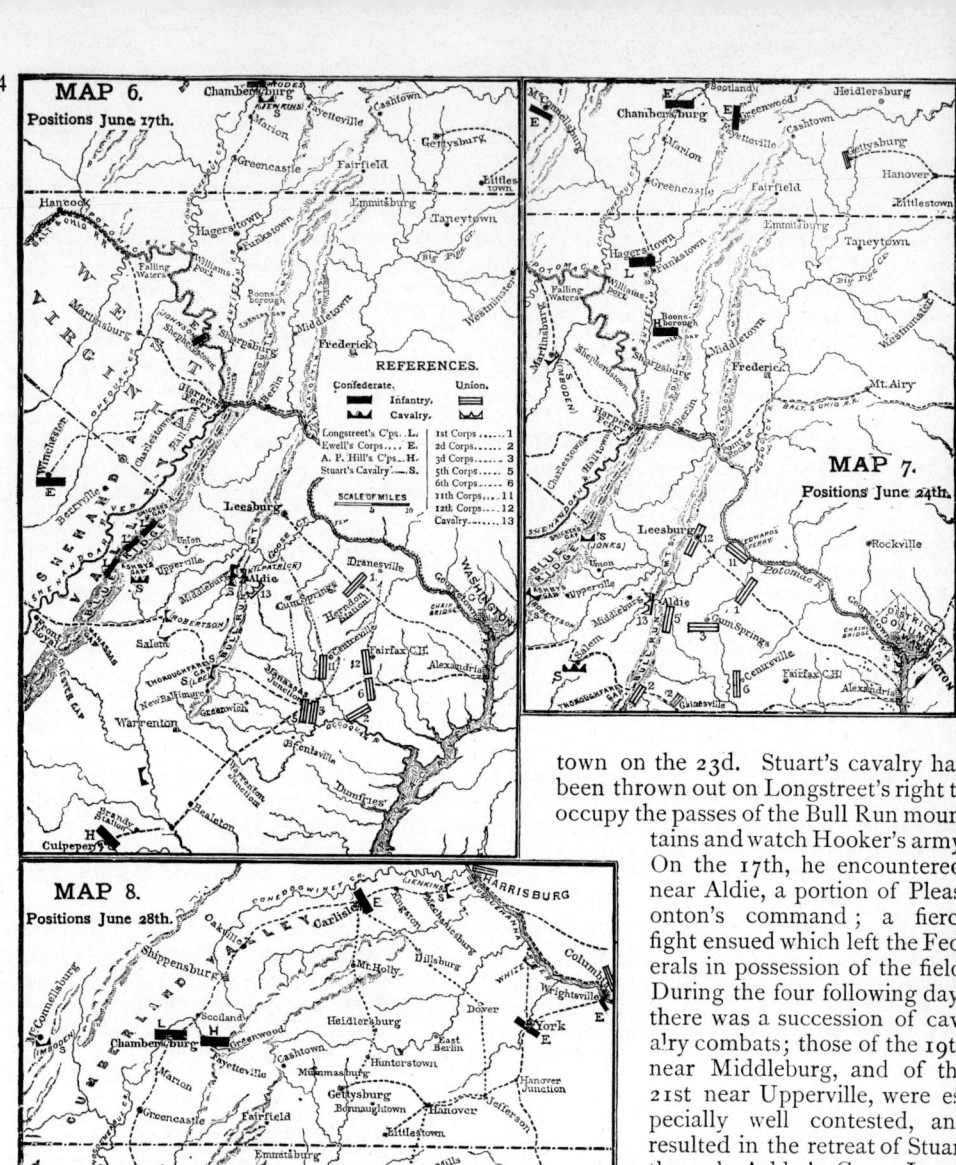

town on the 23d. Stuart's cavalry had been thrown out on Longstreet's right to occupy the passes of the Bull Run mountains and watch Hooker's army. On the 17th, he encountered near Aldie, a portion of Pleasonton's command; a fierce fight ensued which left the Federals in possession of the field. During the four following days there was a succession of cavalry combats; those of the 19th near Middleburg, and of the 21st near Upperville, were especially well contested, and resulted in the retreat of Stuart through Ashby's Gap. Longstreet had already withdrawn through the gaps and followed Hill to the Potomac. Imboden, his work of destruction completed, had taken post at Hancock. Longstreet and Hill crossed the Potomac on the 24th and 25th and directed their march on Chambersburg and Fayetteville, arriving on the 27th. Stuart had been directed to guard the mountain passes until the Federal army crossed the river, and, according to General Lee's report, "to lose no time in placing his command on the right of our [Confederate] column as soon as he should perceive the enemy moving northward," in order to

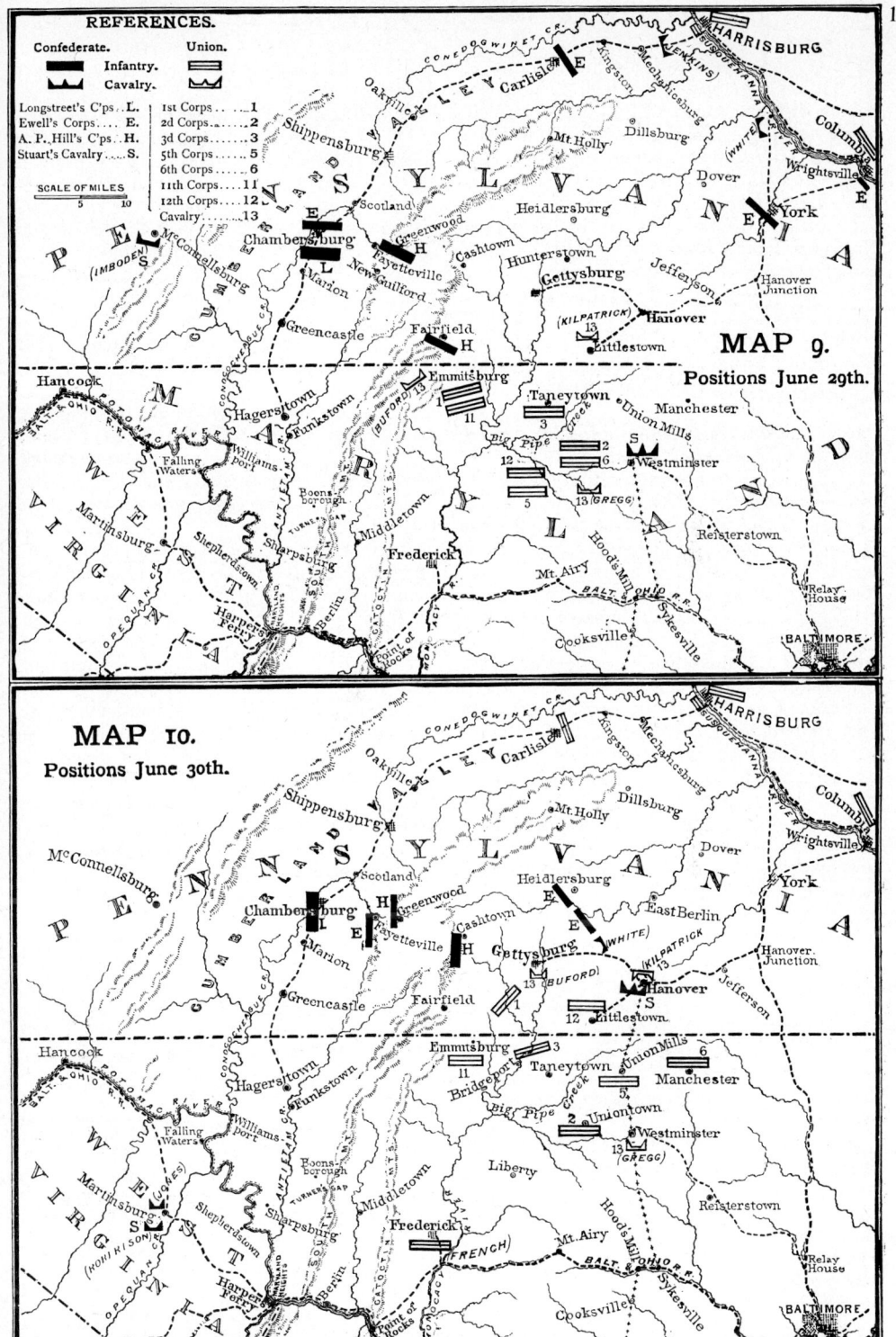

watch and report his movements. According to Stuart's report, he was authorized to cross between the Federal army and Washington, and directed after crossing to proceed with all dispatch to join Early in Pennsylvania.

General Lee so far had been completely successful; his army was exultant, and he lost no time in availing himself of his advantages. On the 21st he ordered Ewell to take possession of Harrisburg; and on the 22d Ewell's whole corps was on the march, Rodes's and Johnson's divisions via Chambersburg to Carlisle, which they reached on the 27th, and Early via Greenwood and Gettysburg to York, with orders from Ewell to break up the Northern Central Railroad, destroy the bridge across the Susquehanna at Wrightsville, and then rejoin the main body at Carlisle. Early entered York on the 28th, and sent Gordon's brigade, not to destroy, but to secure possession of the bridge, which would enable him to operate upon Harrisburg from the rear; but a small militia force under Colonel Frick, retreating from Wrightsville across the bridge, after an unsuccessful attempt to destroy one of its spans, set fire to and entirely destroyed that fine structure, Gordon's troops giving their aid to the citizens to save the town from the flames. On the 29th, Ewell received orders from General Lee to rejoin the army at Cashtown; the next evening, 30th, his reserve artillery and trains, with Johnson's division as an escort, were near Chambersburg, and Ewell, with Early's, and Rodes's, near Heidlersburg. Thus suddenly ended Ewell's Harrisburg expedition. One object was to collect supplies, and contributions were accordingly levied. Much damage was done to roads and bridges, but the prompt advance of the Army of the Potomac made this useless to the Confederates.

Before committing his army to an invasion of the North, General Lee recommended the proper steps to cover and support it. In a letter of June 23d, addressed to President Davis, he states that the season was so far advanced as to stop further Federal operations on the Southern coast, and that Confederate troops in that country and elsewhere were now disposable. He proposed, therefore, that an army should as soon as possible be organized at Culpeper, as "the well-known anxiety of the Northern Government for the safety of its capital would induce it to retain a large force for its defense, and thus relieve the opposition to our advance"; and suggested that General Beauregard be placed in command, "as his presence would give magnitude even to a small demonstration." On the 25th, he wrote twice to Mr. Davis urging the same views. The proposition embarrassed Mr. Davis, who could not see how, with the few troops under his hand, it could be carried out. In fact, although General Lee had pointed out the means, the proposition came too late, as the decisive battle took place much earlier than was expected. This correspondence, however, with that between General Lee and Mr. Seddon, shows that Hooker's project to capture Richmond by a *coup-de-main* was feasible.

It was not now a question of "swapping queens." Washington was safe, being well fortified and sufficiently garrisoned, or with available troops within reach, without drawing on Hooker; and to take Richmond and scatter the Confederate Government was the surest way to ruin Lee's army — " his true objective."

On the first appearance of danger of invasion, her vigilant governor, Curtin, warned the people of Pennsylvania, and called out the militia. General Couch was sent to Harrisburg to organize and command them, but disbelief in the danger — due to previous false alarms — caused delays until the fugitives from Milroy's command, followed by Jenkins's cavalry, roused the country. Defensive works were then thrown up at Harrisburg and elsewhere, and local forces were raised and moved toward the enemy.

Early in June, General Hooker represented in strong terms the necessity of having one commander for all the troops whose operations would have an influence on those of Lee's army, and in reply was informed by General Halleck that any movements he might suggest for other commands than his own would be ordered *if practicable*. Misunderstandings and confusion naturally resulted from such an arrangement, and authority was given him from time to time to exercise control over the troops of Heintzelman, commanding the Department of Washington, and of Schenck commanding the Middle Department, followed, June 24th, by orders specifically placing the troops in Harper's Ferry and its vicinity at his disposal.

Disregarding Ewell's movements, Hooker conformed his own to those of the enemy's main body, and crossed the Potomac at Edwards's Ferry on the 25th and 26th of June. On the 27th, three army-corps under Reynolds occupied Middletown and the South Mountain passes. The Twelfth Corps was near Harper's Ferry, and the three other corps at or near Frederick. Hooker now ordered the Twelfth Corps to march early on the 28th to Harper's Ferry, there to be joined by its garrison from Maryland Heights, in order to cut Lee's communications with Virginia, and in conjunction with Reynolds to operate on his rear. General Halleck, however, objected to the abandonment of the Heights, notwithstanding Hooker's representations that the position was utterly useless for any purpose; whereupon Hooker abandoned his project, and finding now that he was "not allowed to manœuvre his own army in the presence of the enemy," asked to be relieved from his command. He had encountered some of the difficulties which

ASSAULT OF BROCKENBROUGH'S CONFEDERATE BRIGADE (HETH'S DIVISION) UPON THE STONE BARN OF THE McPHERSON FARM.

The line of the stone barn was held by Stone's brigade, Pennsylvania Bucktails (Doubleday's division), its right resting on the Chambersburg pike (the left of the picture) and its left on the McPherson woods (right background of the picture), where a part of Archer's Confederate brigade of Heth's division was captured by Meredith's brigade.— EDITOR.

had beset a predecessor whom he had himself mercilessly criticised, and promptly succumbed to them. His request was complied with, and Major-General George G. Meade was appointed his successor, this being the fifth change of commanders of the Army of the Potomac in ten months. General Meade was an excellent officer of long service, who had always proved equal to his position, whether as a specialist or a commander of troops. Many welcomed his advent — some regretted Hooker. All thought the time for the change unfortunate, but accepted loyally, as the Army of the Potomac ever did, the leader designated by the President, and gave him their hearty support. He was succeeded in the command of the Fifth Corps by Major-General George Sykes, a veteran of the Mexican war and a distinguished soldier.

When General Meade assumed command, June 28th, the best information placed Longstreet at Chambersburg, A. P. Hill between that place and Cashtown, and Ewell in occupation of Carlisle, York, and the country between them, threatening Harrisburg. Unacquainted with Hooker's plans and views, he determined at once to move on the main line from Frederick to Harrisburg, extending his wings as far as compatible with a ready concentration, in order to force Lee to battle before he could cross the Susquehanna. With this view he spent the day in ascertaining the position of his army, and brought up his cavalry, Buford to his left, Gregg to his right, and Kilpatrick to the front. Directing French to occupy Frederick with seven thousand men of the garrison of Harper's Ferry, he put his army in motion early on the morning of the 29th. Kilpatrick reached Littlestown that night; and on the morning of the 30th, the rear of his division, while passing through Hanover, was attacked by a portion of Stuart's cavalry. Stuart, availing himself of the discretion allowed him, had left Robertson's and Jones's brigades to guard the passes of the Blue Ridge, and on the night of the 24th, with those of Hampton, Fitzhugh Lee and Chambliss, had started to move round the Army of the Potomac, pass between it and Centreville into Maryland, and so rejoin Lee; but the movements of that army forced him so far east that he was compelled to ford the Potomac near Seneca, on the night of the 27th. Next morning, learning that Hooker had already crossed the river, he marched north by Rockville, where he captured a wagon train. Paroling his prisoners and taking the train with him, he pushed on—through Westminster, where he had a sharp action with a squadron of Delaware horse—to Union Mills, and encamped there on the 29th. During the night, he learned that the Federal army was still between him and Lee on its march north, and his scouts reported its cavalry in strong force at Littlestown, barring his direct road to Gettysburg; wherefore, on the morning of the 30th he moved across country to Hanover, Chambliss in front and Hampton in rear of his long train of two hundred wagons, with Fitzhugh Lee well out on his left flank. About 10 A. M. Chambliss, reaching Hanover, found Kilpatrick passing through the town and attacked him, but was driven out before Hampton or Lee could come to his support. Stuart's men and horses were now nearly worn out; he was encumbered with a large captured train; a junction with some part of Lee's army was a necessity, and he made a night march for York, only to learn that Early had left the day before. Pushing on to Carlisle, he found that Ewell was gone, and the place occupied by a militia force under General W. F. Smith. His demand of a surrender was refused, upon which he threw a few shells into the town and burned the Government barracks.

That night he learned that Lee's army was concentrating at Gettysburg, and left for that place next day. Thus ended a "raid" which greatly embarrassed General Lee, and by which the services of three fine cavalry brigades were, in the critical period of the campaign, exchanged for a few hundred prisoners and a wagon train.

Hearing nothing from Stuart, and therefore believing that Hooker was still south of the Potomac, Lee, on the afternoon of the 28th, ordered Longstreet and Hill to join Ewell at Harrisburg; but late that night one of Longstreet's scouts came in and reported that the Federal army had crossed the river, that Meade had relieved Hooker and was at Frederick. Lee thereupon changed the rendezvous of his army to Cashtown, which place Heth reached on the 29th, and next day sent Pettigrew's brigade on to Gettysburg, nine miles, to procure a supply of shoes. Nearing this place, Pettigrew discovered the advance of a large Federal force and returned to Cashtown. Hill immediately notified Generals Lee and Ewell, informing the latter that he would advance next morning on Gettysburg. Buford, sending Merritt's brigade to Mechanicstown as guard to his trains, had early on the morning of the 29th crossed into and moved up the Cumberland valley via Boonsboro' and Fairfield with those of Gamble and Devin, and on the afternoon of Tuesday, June 30th, under instructions from Pleasonton, entered Gettysburg, Pettigrew's brigade withdrawing on his approach.

From Gettysburg, near the eastern base of the Green Ridge, and covering all the upper passes into the Cumberland valley, good roads lead to all important points between the Susquehanna and the Potomac. It is therefore an important strategic position. On the west of the town, distant nearly half a mile, there is a somewhat elevated ridge running north and south, on which stands the "Lutheran Seminary." It is covered with open woods through its whole length,[7] and is terminated nearly a mile and a half north of the seminary by a commanding knoll, bare on its southern side, called Oak Hill. From this ridge the ground slopes gradually to the west, and again rising forms another ridge about five hundred yards from the first, upon which, nearly opposite the seminary, stands McPherson's farm buildings. This second ridge is wider, smoother, and lower than the first, and Oak Hill, their intersection, has a clear view of the slopes of both ridges and of the valley between them. West of McPherson's ridge Willoughby Run flows south into Marsh Creek. South of the farm buildings and directly opposite the seminary, a wood borders the run for about three hundred yards, and stretches back to the summit of McPherson's ridge. From the town two roads run; one south-west to Hagerstown via Fairfield, the other north-westerly via Chambersburg via Cashtown. The seminary is midway between them, about three hundred yards from each. Parallel to, and one hundred and fifty yards north of the Chambersburg pike, is the bed of an unfinished railroad, with deep cuttings through the two ridges. Directly north of the town the country is comparatively flat and open; on the east of it, Rock Creek flows south. On the south, and overlooking it, is a ridge of bold, high grounds, terminated on the west by Cemetery Hill and on the east by Culp's Hill, which, bending to the south, extends half a mile or more and terminates in low grounds near Spangler's Spring. Culp's Hill is steep toward the east, is well wooded, and its eastern base is washed by Rock Creek.

Impressed by the importance of the position, Buford, expecting the early return of the enemy in force, assigned to Devin's brigade the country north, and to Gamble's that west of the town; sent out scouting parties on all the roads to collect information, and reported the condition of affairs to Reynolds. His pickets extended from below the Fairfield road, along the eastern bank of Willoughby Run, to the railroad cut, then easterly some fifteen hundred yards north of the town, to a wooded hillock near Rock Creek.

THE BATTLE OF THE FIRST DAY AT GETTYSBURG.

CONFEDERATE DEAD GATHERED FOR BURIAL NEAR THE McPHERSON WOODS. (FROM PHOTOGRAPHS.) 8

ing the general line of Pipe Creek as a suitable locality. Carefully drawn instructions were sent to the corps commanders as to the occupation of this line, should it be ordered; but it was added that developments might cause the offensive to be assumed from present positions. These orders were afterward cited as indicating General Meade's intention not to fight at Gettysburg. They were, under any circumstances, wise and proper orders, and it would probably have been better had he concentrated his army behind Pipe Creek

On the night of June 30th Meade's headquarters and the Reserve artillery were at Taneytown; the First Corps at Marsh Run, the Eleventh at Emmettsburg, Third at Bridgeport, Twelfth at Littlestown, Second at Uniontown, Fifth at Union Mills, Sixth and Gregg's cavalry at Manchester, Kilpatrick's at Hanover. A glance at the map (page 15) will show at what disadvantage Meade's army was now placed. Lee's whole army was nearing Gettysburg, whilst that of Meade was scattered over a wide extent of country to the east and south of that town.

Meade was now convinced that all designs on the Susquehanna had been abandoned; but as Lee's corps were reported as occupying the country from Chambersburg to Carlisle, he ordered for the next day's moves, the First and Eleventh Corps to Gettysburg, under Reynolds, the Third to Emmettsburg, Second to Taneytown, Fifth to Hanover, and the Twelfth to Two Taverns, directing Slocum to take command of the Fifth in addition to his own. The Sixth Corps was left at Manchester, thirty-four miles from Gettysburg, to await orders. But Meade, while conforming to the current of Lee's movement, was not merely drifting. That same afternoon he directed the chiefs of engineers and artillery to select a field of battle on which his army might be concentrated, whatever Lee's lines of approach, whether by Harrisburg or Gettysburg, indicat- rather than at Gettysburg; but events finally controlled the actions of both leaders.

At 8 A. M., July 1st, Buford's scouts reported Heth's advance on the Cashtown road, when Gamble's brigade formed on McPherson's Ridge, from the Fairfield road to the railroad cut; one section of Calef's battery A, Second United States, near the left of his line,[9] the other two across the Chambersburg or Cashtown pike. Devin formed his disposable squadrons from Gamble's right toward Oak Hill, from which he had afterward to transfer them to the north of the town to meet Ewell. As Heth advanced, he threw Archer's brigade to the right, Davis's to the left of the Cashtown pike, with Pettigrew's and Brockenbrough's brigades in support. The Confederates advanced skirmishing heavily with Buford's dismounted troopers. Calef's battery engaging double the number of its own guns,[10] was served with an efficiency worthy of its ancient reputation as "Duncan's battery" in the Mexican

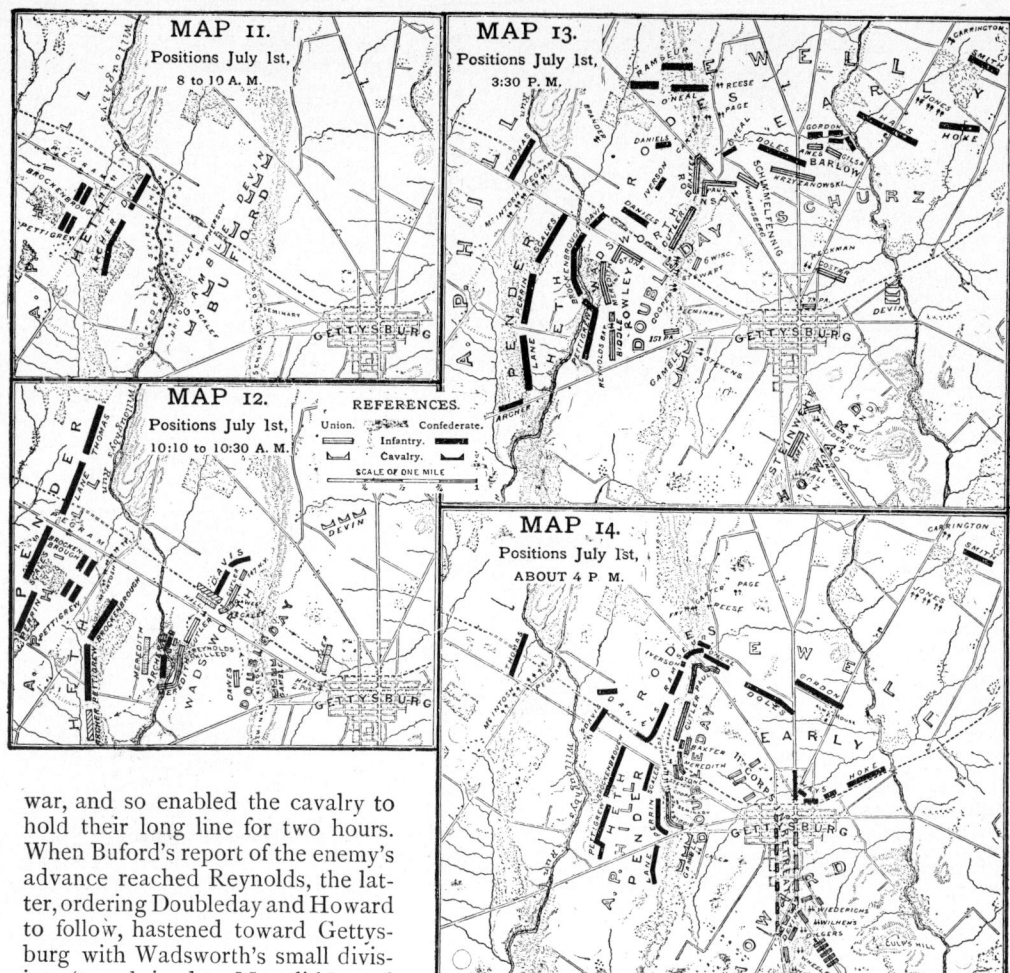

war, and so enabled the cavalry to hold their long line for two hours. When Buford's report of the enemy's advance reached Reynolds, the latter, ordering Doubleday and Howard to follow, hastened toward Gettysburg with Wadsworth's small division (two brigades, Meredith's and Cutler's) and Hall's Second Maine battery. As he approached he heard the sound of battle, and directing the troops to cross the fields toward the firing, galloped himself to the seminary, met Buford there, and both rode to the front, where the cavalry, dismounted, were gallantly holding their ground against heavy odds. After viewing the field, he sent back to hasten up Howard, and as the enemy's main line was now advancing to the attack, directed Doubleday, who had arrived in advance of his division, to look to the Fairfield road, sent Cutler with three of his five regiments north of the railroad cut, posted the other two under Colonel Fowler, of the Fourteenth New York, south of the pike, and replaced Calef's battery by Hall's; thus relieving the cavalry. Cutler's line was hardly formed when it was struck by Davis's brigade on its front and right flank, whereupon Wadsworth, to save it, ordered it to fall back to Seminary Ridge. This order not reaching the One Hundred and Forty-seventh New York, its gallant Major, Harney, held that regiment to its position until, having lost half its numbers, the order to retire was repeated. Hall's battery was now imperiled, and it withdrew by sections, fighting at close canister range and suffering severely. Fowler thereupon changed his front to face Davis's brigade, which held the cut, and with Dawes's Sixth Wisconsin,— sent by Doubleday to aid the One Hundred and Forth-seventh New York,— charged and drove Davis from the field. The Confederate brigade suffered severely, losing all its field officers but two, and a large proportion of its men killed and captured, disabling it for further effective service on that day. In the meantime, Archer's Confederate brigade had occupied McPherson's wood, and as the regiments of Meredith's "Iron Brigade" came up, they were sent forward by Doubleday, who fully recognized the importance of the position, to dislodge it. At the entrance of the wood they found Reynolds in person, and, animated by his presence, rushed to the charge, struck successive heavy blows, outflanked and turned the enemy's right, captured General Archer and a large portion of his brigade, and pursued the remainder across Willoughby Run. Wadsworth's small division had thus won decided successes against superior numbers, but it was at grievous cost to the army and the country, for Reynolds, whilst directing the operations, was killed in the wood by a sharp-shooter. It was not, however, until he had by his promptitude and gallantry determined the decisive field of the war, and brilliantly opened a battle which required three days of hard fighting to close with a victory. To him may be applied in a wider sense than in its original one, Napier's happy eulogium on Ridge: No man died on that field with more glory than he, yet many died, and there was much glory.[11]

After the repulse of Davis and Archer, Heth's division was formed in line mostly south of the Cashtown pike, with Pender's in second line, Pegram's and McIntosh's artillery (nine batteries) occupying all the commanding positions west of Willoughby Run; Doubleday reëstablished his former lines, Meredith holding McPherson's wood. Soon after, Rowley's and Robinson's divisions (two brigades each) and the four remaining batteries of the corps arrived. Rowley's division was thrown forward, Stone's brigade to the interval between Meredith and Cutler, and Biddle's with Cooper's battery to occupy the ridge between the wood and the Fairfield road. Reynolds's battery replaced Hall's, and Calef's rejoined Gamble's cavalry, now in reserve. Robinson's division was halted near the base of Seminary Ridge. By this time, near noon, General Howard arrived, assumed command, and directed General Schurz, commanding the Eleventh Corps, to prolong Doubleday's line toward Oak Hill with Schimmelpfennig's and Barlow's divisions and three batteries, and to post Steinwehr's division and two batteries on Cemetery Hill, as a rallying point. By one o'clock, when this corps was arriving, Buford had reported Ewell's approach by the Heidlersburg road, and Howard called on Sickles at Emmettsburg and Slocum at Two Taverns for aid, to which both these officers promptly responded. It was now no longer a question of prolonging Doubleday's line, but of protecting it against Ewell whilst engaged in front with Hill. Schurz's two divisions, hardly six thousand effectives, accordingly formed line on the open plain, half a mile north of the town. They were too weak to cover the ground, and a wide interval was left between the two corps, covered only by the fire of Dilger's and Wheeler's batteries (ten guns) posted behind it.

That morning, whilst on the march to Cashtown, Ewell received Hill's notice that his corps was advancing to Gettysburg, upon which he turned the heads of his own columns

GRAVE OF CONFEDERATE DEAD ON THE FIELD OF THE FIRST DAY. (FROM A PHOTOGRAPH.)

to that point. Reporting the change by a staff-officer to General Lee, Ewell was instructed that if the Federals were in force at Gettysburg a general battle was not to be brought on until the rest of the army was up. Approaching Gettysburg, Rodes, guided by the sounds of battle, followed the prolongation of Seminary Ridge; Iverson's, Daniel's, and Ramseur's brigades on the western, O'Neal's and Doles's on the eastern slope. Ewell, recognizing the importance of Oak Hill, ordered it to be occupied by Carter's artillery

THE LINE OF DEFENSE AT THE CEMETERY GATE-HOUSE. (FROM A PHOTOGRAPH.)

battalion, which immediately opened on both the Federal corps, enfilading Doubleday's line. This caused Wadsworth again to withdraw Cutler to Seminary Ridge, and Reynolds's battery was posted near McPherson's house, under partial cover. Stone therefore placed two of his three regiments on the Cashtown pike, so as to face Oak Hill. This left an interval between Stone and Cutler, through which Cooper and Reynolds could fire with effect, and gave to these lines a cross-fire on troops entering the angle between them. Robinson now sent his two brigades to strengthen Cutler's right. They took post behind the stone walls of a field, Paul's brigade facing west, Baxter's north. Rodes, regarding this advance as a menace, gave orders at 2:30 P. M. to attack. Iverson, sweeping round to his left, engaged Paul, who prolonged Cutler's line, and O'Neal attacked Baxter. The repulse of O'Neal soon enabled Baxter to turn upon Iverson. Cutler also attacked him in flank, and after losing five hundred men killed and wounded, three of Iverson's regiments surrendered. General Robinson reports the capture of one thousand prisoners and three colors; General Paul was severely wounded, losing both eyes. Meanwhile Daniel's brigade advanced directly on Stone, who maintained his lines against this attack and also Brockenbrough's, of Hill's corps, but was soon severely wounded. Colonel Wister, who succeeded him, met the same fate, and Colonel Dana took command of the brigade. Ramseur, who followed Daniel, by a conversion to the left now faced Robinson and Cutler with his own brigade, the remnant of Iverson's, and one regiment of O'Neal's,

his right connecting with Daniel's left, and the fighting was hot. East of the Ridge, Doles's brigade had been held in observation, but about 3:30 P. M., on the advance of Early, he sent his skirmishers forward and drove those of Devin's — who had gallantly held the enemy's advance in check with his dismounted troopers — from their line and its hillock on Rock Creek. Barlow, considering this an eligible position for his own right, advanced his division, supported by Wilkeson's battery, and seized it. This made it necessary for Schurz to advance a brigade of Schimmelpfennig's division to connect with Barlow, thus lengthening his already too extended line.

The arrival of Early's division had by this time brought an overwhelming force on the flank and rear of the Eleventh Corps. On the east of Rock Creek, Jones's artillery battalion, within easy range, enfiladed its whole line and took it in reverse, while the brigades of Gordon, Hays, and Avery in line, with Smith's in reserve, advanced about four P. M. upon Barlow's position, Doles, of Rodes's division, connecting with Gordon. An obstinate and bloody contest ensued, in which Barlow was desperately wounded, Wilkeson killed, and the whole corps forced back to its original line, on which, with the aid of Coster's brigade and Heckman's battery, drawn from Cemetery Hill, Schurz endeavored to rally it and cover the town. The fighting here was well sustained, but the Confederate force was overpowering in numbers, and the troops retreated to Cemetery Hill, Ewell entering the town about 4:30 P. M. These retrograde movements had uncovered the flank of the First Corps and made its right untenable.

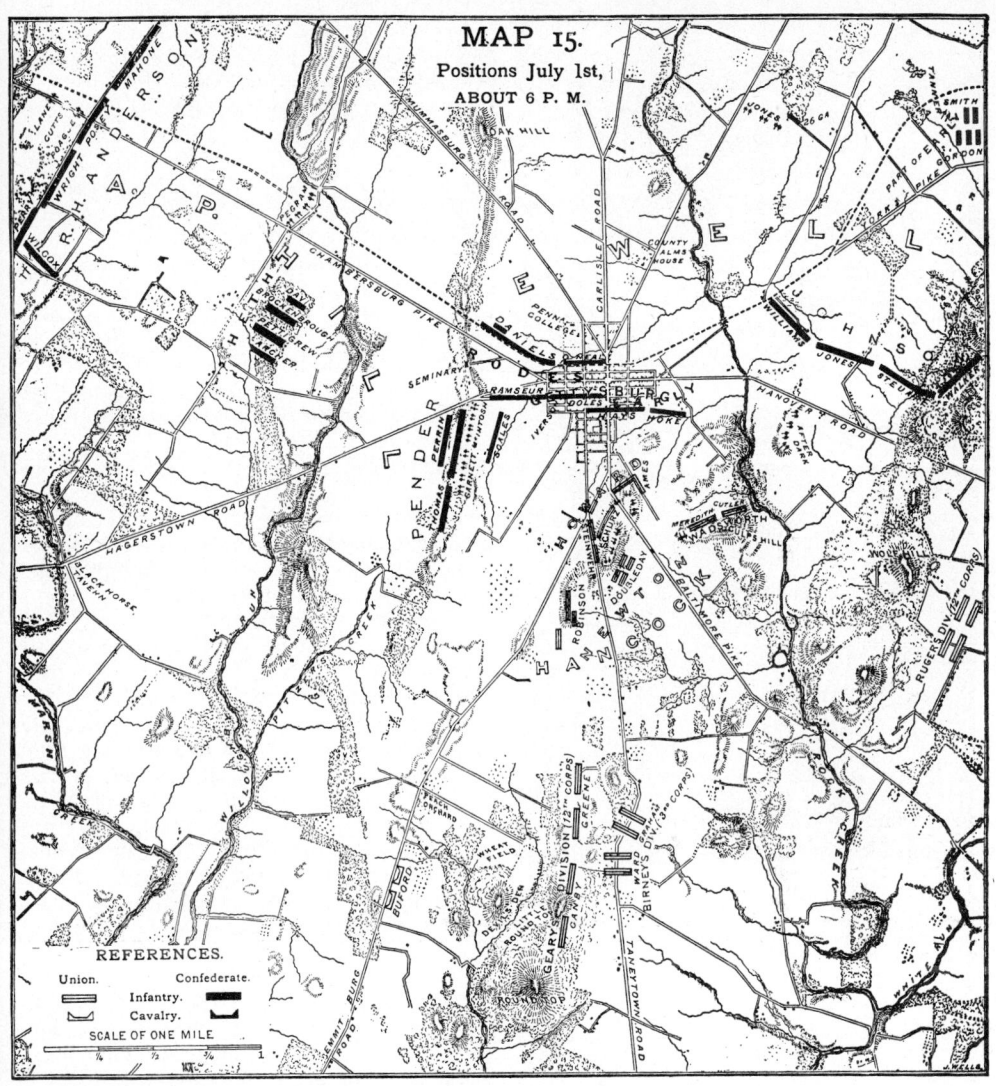

Meanwhile, that corps had been heavily engaged along its whole line; for, on the approach of Rodes, Hill attacked with both his divisions. There were thus opposed to the single disconnected Federal line south of the Cashtown pike two solid Confederate ones which outflanked their left a quarter of a mile or more. Biddle's small command, less than one thousand men, after a severe contest, was gradually forced back. In McPherson's wood and beyond, Meredith's and Dana's brigades repeatedly repulsed their assailants, but as Biddle's retirement uncovered their left, they too fell back to successive positions from which they inflicted heavy losses, until finally all three reached the foot of Seminary Ridge, where Colonel Wainwright, commanding the corps artillery, had planted twelve guns south of the Cashtown pike, with Stewart's battery, manned in part by men of the Iron Brigade, north of it. Buford had already thrown half of Gamble's dismounted men south of the Fairfield road. Heth's division had suffered so severely that Pender's had passed to its front, thus bringing fresh troops to bear on the exhausted Federal line.

It was about four P. M. when the whole Confederate line advanced to the final attack. On their right Gamble held Lane's brigade for some time in check, Perrin's and Scales's suffered severely, and Scales's was broken up, for Stewart, swinging half his guns, under Lieutenant Davison, upon the Cashtown pike, raked it. The whole corps being now heavily

JOHN L. BURNS, "THE OLD HERO OF GETTYSBURG."
(FROM A PHOTOGRAPH TAKEN SOON AFTER THE BATTLE.)

In his official report, General Doubleday says: "My thanks are specially due to a citizen of Gettysburg named John Burns, who, although over seventy years of age, shouldered his musket and offered his services to Colonel Wister, 150th Pennsylvania Volunteers. Colonel Wister advised him to fight in the woods, as there was more shelter there; but he preferred to join our line of skirmishers in the open fields. When the troops retired, he fought with the Iron Brigade. He was wounded in three places."

pressed and its right uncovered, Doubleday gave the order to fall back to Cemetery Hill, which was effected in comparatively good order, the rear, covered by the Seventh Wisconsin, turning when necessary to check pursuit. Colonel Wainwright, mistaking the order, had clung with his artillery to Seminary Hill, until, seeing the infantry retreating to the town, he moved his batteries down the Cashtown pike until lapped on both sides by the enemy's skirmishers, at close range, when they were compelled to abandon one gun on the road,[12] all its horses being killed. The Eleventh Corps also left a disabled gun on the field.[13] Of the troops who passed through the town, many got entangled in the streets, lost their way, and were captured, principally men of the Eleventh Corps.

On ascending Cemetery Hill, the retreating troops found Steinwehr's division in position covered by stone fences on the slopes, and occupying by their skirmishers the houses in front of their line. As they arrived they were formed, the Eleventh Corps on the right, the First Corps on the left of Steinwehr. As the batteries came up, they were well posted by Colonels Wainwright and Osborn, and soon a formidable array of artillery was ready to cover with its fire all the approaches. Buford assembled his command on the plain west of Cemetery Hill, covering the left flank and presenting a firm front to any attempt at pursuit. The First Corps found a small reënforcement awaiting it, in the Seventh Indiana, part of the train escort which brought up nearly five hundred fresh men. General Wadsworth met and led them to Culp's Hill, where, under direction of Captain Pattison of that regiment, a defensive line was marked out. Their brigade (Cutler's) soon joined them; wood and stone were plentiful, and soon the right of the line was solidly established.

Nor was there wanting other assurance to the men who had fought so long that their sacrifices had not been in vain. As they reached the hill they were received by General Hancock, who arrived just as they were coming up from the town, under orders from General Meade to assume the command. His person was well known; his presence inspired confidence, and it implied also the near approach of his army-corps. Ordering Wadsworth at once to Culp's Hill to secure that important position,—an excellent selection,— and aided by Howard, and Warren who had also just arrived from headquarters, and others, a strong line, well flanked, was soon formed.

General Lee, who had from Seminary Hill witnessed the final attack, sent Colonel Long, of his staff, a competent officer of sound judgment, to examine the position, and directed Ewell to carry it if practicable, renewing, however, his previous warning to avoid bringing on a general engagement until the army was all up. Both Ewell, who was making some preparations with a view to attack, and Long found the position a formidable one, strongly occupied, and not accessible to artillery fire. Ewell's men were indeed in no condition for an immediate assault. Of Rodes's eight thousand, nearly three thousand were *hors de combat*. Early had lost over five hundred, and had but two brigades disposable, the other two having been sent on the report of the advance of Federal troops, probably the Twelfth Corps, then near by, to watch the York road. Hill's two divisions had been very roughly handled, had lost heavily, and he withdrew them to Seminary Hill as Ewell entered the town,

THE BATTLE OF THE FIRST DAY AT GETTYSBURG. 25

leaving the latter without more than eight thousand men to secure the town and the prisoners. Ewell's absent division was expected soon, but it did not arrive until near sunset, when the Twelfth Federal Corps and Stannard's Vermont brigade were also up, and the Third Corps arriving. In fact an assault by the Confederates was not practicable before 5:30 P. M., and after that the position was perfectly secure. For the first time that day the Federals had the advantage of position, and sufficient troops and artillery to occupy it, and General Ewell would not have been justified in attacking without the positive orders of General Lee, who was present, and wisely abstained from giving them.

MENCHEY'S SPRING, BETWEEN CULP'S HILL AND THE CEMETERY GATE.
(BOTH DRAWINGS ARE AFTER SKETCHES BY C. W. REED.)

SPANGLER'S SPRING, EAST OF CULP'S HILL.

THE SECOND DAY AT GETTYSBURG.

ON June 30th General Meade at Taneytown received information that the enemy was advancing on Gettysburg, and corps commanders were at once instructed to hold their commands in readiness to march against him. The next day, July 1st, Meade wrote to Reynolds that telegraphic intelligence from Couch, and the movements reported by Buford, indicated a concentration of the enemy's army either at Chambersburg, or at some point on a line drawn from that place through Heidlersburg to York. Under these circumstances, Meade informed Reynolds that he had not yet decided whether it was his best policy to move to attack before he knew more definitely Lee's point of concentration. He seems, however, soon to have determined not to advance until the movements or position of the enemy gave strong assurance of success; and that if the enemy took the offensive, he would withdraw his own army from its actual positions and form line of battle behind Pipe Creek, between Middleburg and Manchester. The considerations probably moving him to this are not difficult to divine. Examination of the map [see The First Day, page 20]

THE "SLAUGHTER PEN" AT THE BASE AND ON THE LEFT SLOPE OF LITTLE ROUND TOP. (FROM PHOTOGRAPHS.)

UNION BREASTWORKS ON LITTLE ROUND TOP — BIG ROUND TOP IN THE DISTANCE.
(FROM WAR-TIME PHOTOGRAPHS.)

tain passes. As Meade believed Lee's army to be at least equal to his own, all the elements of the problem were in favor of the Pipe Creek line. But Meade's orders for July 1st, drawing his corps towards the threatened flank, carried Reynolds to will show that such a line would cover Baltimore and Washington in all directions from which Lee could advance and that Westminster, his depot, would be immediately behind him, with short railroad communication to Baltimore. It would, moreover, save much hard marching, and restore to the ranks the thousands of stragglers who did not reach Gettysburg.

From Westminster—which is in Parr's Ridge, the eastern boundary of the valley of the Monocacy— good roads led in all directions, and gave the place the same strategic value for Meade that Gettysburg had for Lee. The new line could not be turned by Lee without imminent danger to his own army, nor could he afford to advance upon Baltimore or Washington, leaving the Army of the Potomac intact behind and so near him; — that would be to invite the fate of Burgoyne. Meade then could safely select a good "offensive-defensive line" behind Pipe Creek and establish himself there, with perfect liberty of action in all directions. Without magazines or assured communications, Lee would have to scatter his army, more or less, in order to subsist it, and so expose it to Meade; or else keep it united, and so starve it, and Meade could compel the latter alternative by simple demonstrations. There would then be but two courses for Lee,— either to attack Meade in his chosen position or to retreat without a battle. The latter, neither the temper of his army nor that of his Government would probably permit. In case of a defeat Meade's line of retreat would be comparatively short, and easily covered, whilst Lee's would be for two marches through an open country before he could gain the moun-

Gettysburg, and Buford's report hastened this movement. Reynolds, who probably never received the Pipe Creek circular, was eager for the conflict, and his collision with Heth assuming the dimension of a battle, caused an immediate concentration of both armies at Gettysburg. Prior to this, the assembling of Meade's army behind Pipe Creek would have been easy, and all fears of injuring thereby the *morale* of his troops were idle; the Army of the Potomac was of "sterner stuff" than that implies. The battle of July 1st changed the situation. Overpowered by numbers, the First and Eleventh corps had, after hard fighting and inflicting as well as incurring heavy losses, been forced back to Cemetery Hill, which they still held. To have withdrawn them now would have been a retreat, and might have discouraged the Federal, as it certainly would have elated the Confederate troops; especially as injurious reports unjust to both the corps named had been circulated. It would have been to acknowledge a defeat when there was no defeat. Meade therefore resolved to fight at Gettysburg. An ominous dispatch from General Halleck to Meade, that afternoon, suggesting that whilst his tactical arrangements were good, his strategy was

GENERAL G. K. WARREN AT THE SIGNAL STATION ON LITTLE ROUND TOP.
(FROM A SKETCH MADE BY A. R. WAUD AT THE TIME.)

at fault, that he was too far east, that Lee might attempt to turn his left, and that Frederick was preferable as a base to Westminster, probably confirmed Meade in this decision.

In pursuance of his instructions, I had that morning (July 1st) reconnoitered the country behind Pipe Creek for a battle-ground. On my return I found General Hancock at General Meade's tent. He informed me that Reynolds was killed, that a battle was going on at Gettysburg, and that he was under orders to proceed to that place. His instructions were to examine it and the intermediate country for a suitable field, and if his report was favorable the troops would be ordered forward. Before the receipt of Hancock's written report from Cemetery Hill, which was not very encouraging, General Meade had received from others information as to the state of affairs at the front, set his troops in motion towards Gettysburg, afterwards urged them to forced marches, and under his orders I gave the necessary instructions to the Artillery Reserve and Park for a battle there. The move was, under the circumstances, a bold one, and Meade, as we will see, took great risks. We left Taneytown towards eleven P. M., and reached Gettysburg after midnight. Soon after, General Meade, accompanied by General Howard and myself, inspected our lines so far as then occupied, after which he directed me to examine them again in the morning, and to see that the artillery was properly posted. He had thus recognized my "command" of the artillery; indeed, he did not know it had been suspended.

I resumed it, therefore, and continued it to the end of the battle.

At the close of July 1st, Johnson's and Anderson's divisions of the Confederate army were up. Ewell's corps now covered our front from Benner's Hill to the Seminary, his line

BRIGADIER-GENERAL STRONG VINCENT, MORTALLY WOUNDED, JULY 2D, IN THE STRUGGLE FOR THE ROUND TOPS.
(FROM A PHOTOGRAPH BY BRADY.)

passing through the town — Johnson on the left, Early in the center, Rodes on the right. Hill's corps occupied Seminary Ridge, and early next morning extended its line from the Seminary south nearly to the Peach Orchard on the Emmettsburg road, Trimble — *vice* Pender,[14] wounded — on the left, Anderson on the right, Pettigrew — *vice* Heth, wounded — in reserve. Of Longstreet's corps, McLaws's division and Hood's — except Law's brigade not yet up — camped that night on Marsh Creek, four miles from Gettysburg. His Reserve Artillery did not reach Gettysburg until nine A. M. of the 2d. Pickett's division had been left at Chambersburg as rear-guard, and joined the corps on the night of the 2d.

It had not been General Lee's intention to deliver a general battle whilst so far from his base unless attacked, but he now found himself by the mere force of circumstances committed to one. If it must take place, the sooner the better. His army was now nearly all on the ground, and delay, whilst it could not improve his own position, would certainly better that of his antagonist. Longstreet, indeed, urged General Lee instead of attacking to turn Meade's left, and by interposing between him and Washington, and threatening his communications, to force him to attack the Confederate army in position; but General Lee probably saw that Meade would be under no such necessity; would have no great difficulty in obtaining supplies, and — disregarding the clamor from Washington — could play a waiting game which it would be impossible for Lee to maintain in the open country. He could not advance on Baltimore or Washington with Meade in his rear, nor could his army subsist itself in a hostile region which would soon swarm with additional enemies. His communications could be cut off, for his recommendation to assemble even a small army at Culpepper to cover them and aid him had not been complied with.

A battle was a necessity to Lee, and a defeat would be more disastrous to Meade, and less so to himself, at Gettysburg than at any point east of it. With the defiles of the South Mountain range close in his rear, which could

MAJOR-GENERAL DANIEL E. SICKLES. (FROM A WAR-TIME PHOTOGRAPH.)

be easily held by a small force, a safe retreat through the Cumberland Valley was assured, so that his army, once through these passes, would be practically on the banks of the Potomac, at a point already prepared for crossing. Any position east of Gettysburg would deprive him of these advantages. It is more probable that General Lee was influenced by cool calculation of this nature than by hot blood, or that the opening success of a chance battle had thrown him off his balance. Whatever his reasons, he decided to accept the gage of battle offered by Meade, and to attack as soon as practicable. Ewell had made arrangements to take possession of Culp's Hill in the early morning, and his troops were under arms for the purpose by the time General Meade had finished the moonlight inspection of his lines, when it was ascertained by a reconnoitering party sent out by Johnson, that the hill was occupied and its defenders on the alert; and further, from a captured dispatch from General Sykes to General Slocum, that the Fifth Corps was on the Hanover road only four miles off, and would march at four A. M. for Culp's Hill. Johnson thereupon deferred his attack and awaited Ewell's instructions.

General Lee had, however, during the night determined to attack the Federal left with Longstreet's corps, and now instructed Ewell, so soon as he heard Longstreet's guns, to make a diversion in his favor, to be converted, if opportunity offered, into a real attack.

Early on the morning of July 2d, when nearly all the Confederate army had reached Gettysburg or its immediate vicinity, a large pecially the night marches, were trying and had caused much straggling.

All this morning Meade was busily engaged personally or by his staff in rectifying his lines, assigning positions to the commands as they came up, watching the enemy, and studying the field, parts of which we have described in general terms, and now refer the reader to the map (page 36) to aid our further description of some necessary even if tedious details. Near the western base of Cemetery Hill is Ziegler's Grove. From this grove the distance nearly due south to the base of the Little Round Top is a mile and a half. A well-defined ridge known as Cemetery Ridge follows this line from Ziegler's for nine hundred yards to another small grove, or clump of trees, where it turns sharply to the east for two hundred

TROSTLE'S FARM, THE SCENE OF THE HARD FIGHTING BY BIGELOW'S NINTH MASSACHUSETTS BATTERY. (FROM A PHOTOGRAPH.)

portion of the Army of the Potomac was still on the road. The Second Corps and Sykes, with two divisions of the Fifth, arrived about seven A. M., Crawford's division not joining until noon; Lockwood's brigade — two regiments from Baltimore — at eight; De Trobriand's and Burling's brigades of the Third Corps, from Emmettsburg, at nine, and the Artillery Reserve and its large ammunition trains from Taneytown at 10:30 A. M. Sedgwick's Sixth Corps, the largest in the army, after a long night march from Manchester, reached Rock Creek at four P. M. The rapidity with which the army was assembled was creditable to it and to its commander. The heat was oppressive, the long marches, es- yards, then turns south again, and continues in a "direct line" towards Round Top, for seven hundred yards, to "George Weikert's." So far the ridge is smooth and open, in full view of Seminary Ridge opposite, and distant from fourteen hundred to sixteen hundred yards. At Weikert's, this ridge is lost in a large body of rocks, hills, and woods, lying athwart the "direct line" to Round Top, and forcing a bend to the east in the Taneytown road. This rough space also stretches for a quarter of a mile or more *west* of this "direct line," towards Plum Run. Towards the south it sinks into low marshy ground which reaches to the base of Little Round Top, half a mile or more from George Weikert's. The west side of this

THE SECOND DAY AT GETTYSBURG.

MONUMENT OF BIGELOW'S NINTH MASSACHUSETTS BATTERY.
(FROM A PHOTOGRAPH BY TIPTON.)

broken ground was wooded through its whole extent from north to south. Between this wood and Plum Run is an open cleared space three hundred yards wide — a continuation of the open country in front of Cemetery Ridge; Plum Run flows south-easterly towards Little Round Top, then makes a bend to the south-west where it receives a small stream or "branch" from Seminary Ridge. In the angle between these streams is Devil's Den, a bold rocky hill, steep on its eastern face, and prolonged as a ridge to the west. It is five hundred yards due west of Little Round Top, and one hundred feet lower. The northern extremity is composed of huge rocks and bowlders, forming innumerable crevices and holes, from the largest of which the hill derives its name. Plum Run valley is here marshy but strewn with similar bowlders, and the slopes of the Round Tops are covered with them. These afforded lurking-places for a multitude of sharp-shooters whom, from the difficulties of the ground, it was impossible to dislodge, and who were opposed by similar methods on our part; so that at the close of the battle these hiding-places, and especially the "Den" itself, were filled with dead and wounded men. This kind of warfare was specially destructive to Hazlett's battery on Round Top, as the cannoneers had to expose themselves in firing, and in one case three were shot in quick succession, before the fourth succeeded in discharging the piece. A cross-road between the Taneytown and Emmettsburg roads runs along the northern base of Devil's Den. From its Plum Run crossing to the Peach Orchard is eleven hundred yards. For the first four hundred yards of this distance, there is a wood on the north and a wheat-field on the south of the road, beyond which the road continues for seven hundred yards to the Emmettsburg road along Devil's Den ridge, which slopes on the north to Plum Run, on the south to Plum "Branch." From Ziegler's Grove the Emmettsburg road runs diagonally across the interval between Cemetery and Seminary ridges, crossing the latter two miles from Ziegler's Grove. From Peach Orchard to Ziegler's is nearly a mile and a half. For half a mile the road runs along a ridge at right angles to that of Devil's Den, which slopes back to Plum Run. The angle at the Peach Orchard is thus formed by the intersection of two bold ridges, one from Devil's Den, the other along the Emmettsburg road. It is distant about six hundred yards from the wood which skirts the whole length of Seminary Ridge and covers the movement of troops between it and Willoughby Run, half a mile beyond. South of the Round Top and Devil's Den ridge the country is open, and the principal obstacles to free movement are the fences — generally of stone — which surround the numerous fields.

TROSTLE'S HOUSE, NEAR WHICH BIGELOW'S BATTERY LOST EIGHTY OUT OF EIGHTY-EIGHT HORSES. (FROM A PHOTOGRAPH.)

VIEW FROM THE POSITION OF HAZLETT'S BATTERY

The monument marks the position of the 91st Pennsylvania of Weed's brigade. The Em
center of Pickett's lines as they charged upon the rid

Looking across the valley of death, from little Round-Top.

LITTLE ROUND TOP. (FROM PHOTOGRAPHS BY TIPTON.)

burg road passes the Peach Orchard, Rogers's, and Codori's; the latter's buildings broke the
tween Cemetery Hill and Little Round Top.— EDITOR.

SICKLES'S POSITION AT THE PEACH ORCHARD, VIEWED FROM THE EMMETTSBURG ROAD LOOKING SOUTH, THE ROUND TOPS ON THE LEFT.

(This and the other outline sketches were made recently by C. W. Reed, who, during the battle, was with Bigelow's Battery.)

As our troops came up they were assigned to places on the line: the Twelfth Corps, General A. S. Williams,— *vice* Slocum, commanding the right wing,— to Culp's Hill, on Wadsworth's right; Second Corps to Cemetery Ridge: Hays's and Gibbon's divisions, from Ziegler's to the clump of trees, Caldwell's to the short ridge to its left and rear. This ridge had been occupied by the Third Corps, which was now directed to prolong Caldwell's line to Round Top, relieving Geary's division, which had been stationed during the night on the extreme left, with two regiments at the base of Little Round Top. The Fifth Corps was placed in reserve near the Rock Creek crossing of the Baltimore pike; the Artillery Reserve and its large trains were parked in a central position on a cross-road from the Baltimore pike to the Taneytown road; Buford's cavalry, except Merritt's brigade at Emmettsburg, was near Round Top, from which it was ordered that morning to Westminster, thus uncovering our left flank; Kilpatrick's and Gregg's divisions were well out on the right flank, from which, after a brush with Stuart on the evening of the 2d, Kilpatrick was sent next morning to replace Buford, Merritt being also ordered up to our left.

The morning was a busy and in some respects an anxious one; it was believed that the whole Confederate army was assembled, that it was equal if not superior to our own in numbers, and that the battle would commence before our troops were up. There was a gap in Slocum's line awaiting a division of infantry, and as some demonstrations of Ewell about daylight indicated an immediate attack at that point, I had to draw batteries from other parts of the line[15]— for the Artillery Reserve was just then starting from Taneytown — to cover it until it could be properly filled. Still there was no hostile movement of the enemy, and General Meade directed Slocum to hold himself in readiness to attack Ewell with the Fifth and Twelfth, so soon as the Sixth Corps arrived. After an examination Slocum reported the ground as unfavorable, in which Warren concurred and advised against an attack there. The project was then abandoned, and Meade postponed all offensive operations until the enemy's intentions should be more clearly developed. In the mean time he took precau-

THE "WHEAT-FIELD."

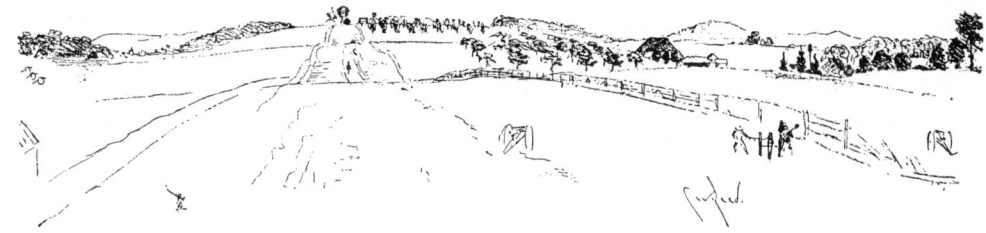

SICKLES'S POSITION AT THE PEACH ORCHARD, VIEWED FROM LONGSTREET'S POSITION ON THE EMMETTSBURG ROAD, LOOKING NORTH.

tionary measures. It was clearly now to his advantage to fight the battle where he was, and he had some apprehension that Lee would attempt to turn his flank, and threaten his communications, just what Longstreet had been advising. In this case it might be necessary to fall back to the Pipe Creek line if possible, or else to follow Lee's movement into the open country. In either case, or in that of a forced withdrawal, prudence dictated that arrangements should be made in advance, and General Meade gave instructions for examining the roads and communications, and to draw up an order of movement which General Butterfield, the chief of staff, seems to have considered an order-absolute for the withdrawal of the army without a battle.

These instructions must have been given early in the morning, for General Butterfield states that it was on his arrival from Taneytown, which place he left at daylight. An order was drawn up accordingly, given to the adjutant-general, and perhaps prepared for issue in case of necessity to corps commanders; but it was not recorded, nor issued, nor even a copy of it preserved. General Meade declared that he never contemplated the issue of such an order unless contingencies made it necessary; and his acts and dispatches during the day were in accordance with his statement. There is one circumstance pertaining to my own duties which to my mind is conclusive, and I relate it because it may have contributed to the idea that General Meade intended to withdraw from Gettysburg. He came to me that morning before the Artillery Reserve had arrived, and, therefore, about the time that the order was in course of preparation, and informed me that one of the army corps had left its whole artillery ammunition train behind it and that others were also deficient, notwithstanding his orders on that subject. He was very much disturbed, and feared that, taking into account the large expenditure of the preceding day by the First and Eleventh Corps, there would not be sufficient to carry us through the battle. This was not the first nor the last time that I was called upon to meet deficiencies under such circumstances, and I was, therefore, prepared for this, having directed General Tyler, commanding the reserve artillery, whatever else he might leave behind, to bring up every round of ammunition in his trains, and I knew he would not fail me. I had, moreover, on my own responsibility, and unknown to General Hooker, formed a special ammunition column, attached to the Artillery Reserve, carrying twenty rounds per gun, over and above the authorized amount, for every gun in the army, in order to meet such emergencies.

SICKLES'S ANGLE AT THE PEACH ORCHARD, AS SEEN FROM THE ROAD LEADING FROM THE WHEAT-FIELD TO THE PEACH ORCHARD.

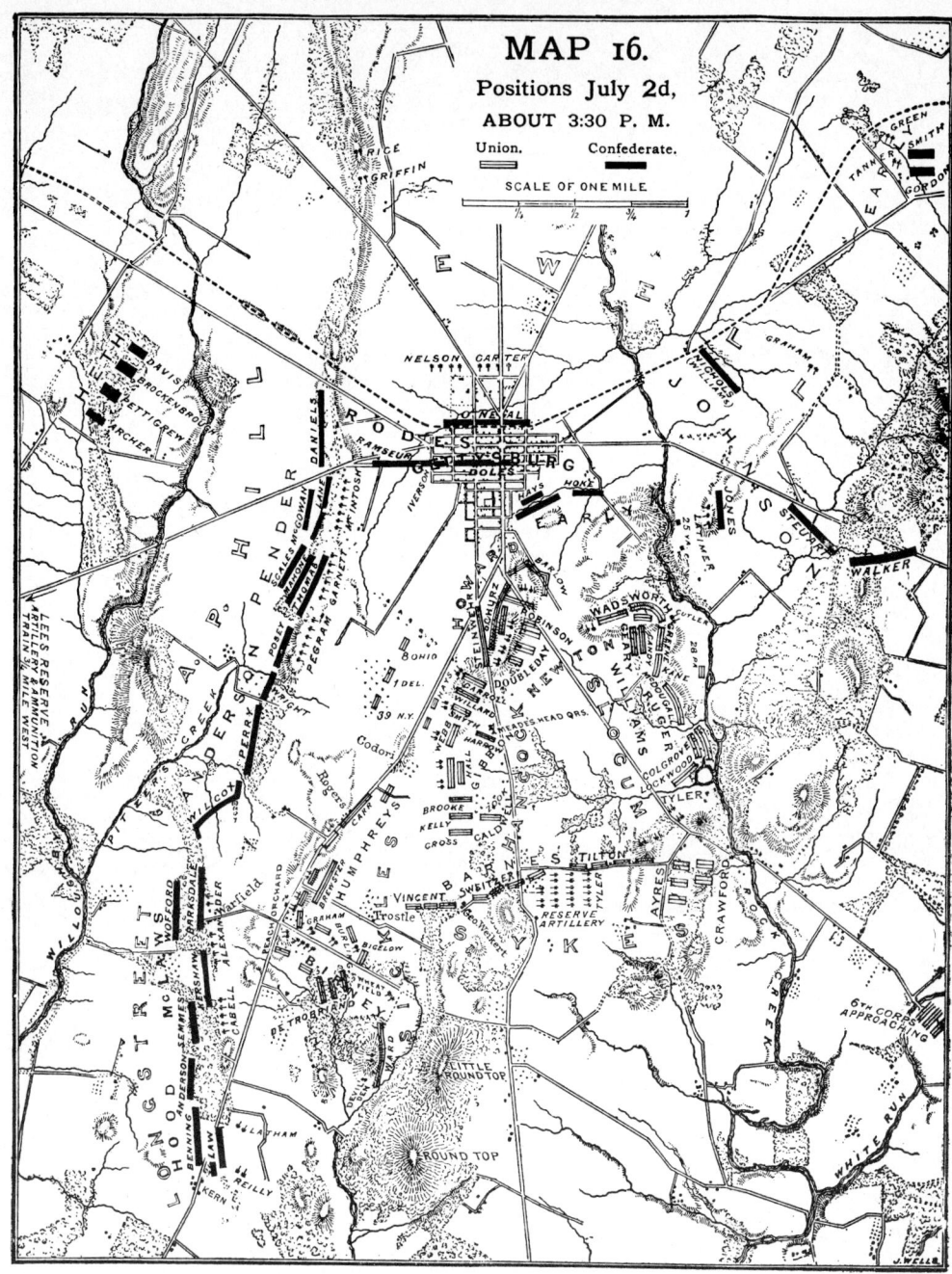

I was therefore able to assure General Meade that there would be enough ammunition for the battle, but none for idle cannonades, the besetting sin of some of our commanders. He was much relieved, and expressed his satisfaction. Now, had he had at this time any intention of withdrawing the army, the first thing to get rid of would have been this Artillery Reserve and its large trains, which were then blocking the roads in our rear; and he would surely have told me of it.[16]

Still, with the exception of occasional cannonading, and some skirmishing near the Peach Orchard, the quiet remained unbroken, although Lee had determined upon an early attack on our left. He says in his detailed report that our line extended "upon the high-ground along the Emmettsburg road, with a steep ridge [Cemetery] in rear which was also occupied"; and in a previous "outline" report he says: "In front of General Longstreet the enemy held a position [the salient angle at the Peach Orchard] from which, if he could be driven, it was thought our artillery could be used to advantage in assailing the more elevated ground beyond, and thus enable us to gain the crest of the ridge." It would appear from this that General Lee mistook the few troops on the Peach Orchard ridge in the morning for our main line, and that by taking it, and sweeping up the Emmettsburg road under cover of his batteries, he expected to "roll up" our lines to Cemetery Hill. That would be an "oblique order of battle," in which the attacking line, formed obliquely to its opponent, marches directly forward, constantly breaking in the *end* of his enemy's line and gaining his rear. General Longstreet was ordered to form the divisions of Hood and McLaws, on Anderson's right, so as to envelop our left and drive it in. These divisions were only three miles off at daylight, and moved early, but there was great delay in forming them for battle, owing principally to the absence of Law's brigade, for which it would have been well to substitute Anderson's fresh division, which could have been replaced by Pettigrew's, then in reserve. There seems to have been no good reason why the attack should not have been made by eight or nine A. M. at the latest, when the Federal Third Corps was not yet all up, nor Crawford's division, nor the Artillery Reserve, nor the Sixth Corps, and our lines still very incomplete. This is one of the cheap criticisms, after all the facts on both sides are known; but it is apt for its purpose, as it shows how great a risk Meade took in abandoning his Pipe Creek line for Gettysburg, on the chances of Lee's army not being yet assembled; and also, that there was no lack of boldness and decision on Meade's part. Indeed his course, from the hour that he took command, had been marked by these qualities.

A suggestive incident is worth recording here. In the course of my inspection of the lines that morning, while passing along Culp's Hill, I found the men hard at work intrenching, and in such fine spirits as at once to attract attention. One of them finally dropped his work, and, approaching me, inquired if the reports just received were true. On asking what he referred to, he replied that twice word had been passed along the line that General McClellan had been assigned to the command of the army, and the second time

OUTLINE SKETCH OF WEED'S POSITION ON LITTLE ROUND TOP, LOOKING IN THE DIRECTION OF THE PEACH ORCHARD.

it was added that he was on the way to the field and might soon be expected. He continued, "The boys are all jubilant over it, for they know that if *he* takes command everything will go right." I have been told recently by the commander of a Fifth Corps battery, that during the forced march of the preceding night the same report ran through that corps, excited great enthusiasm amongst the men, and renewed their vigor. It was probably from this corps — just arrived — that the report had spread along the line.[17]

On my return to headquarters from this inspection General Meade told me that General Sickles, then with him, wished me to examine a new line, as he thought that assigned to him was not a good one, especially that he could not use his artillery there. I had been as far as Round Top that morning, noticed the unfavorable character of the ground, and, therefore, accompanied Sickles direct to the Peach Orchard, where he pointed out the ridges, already described, as his proposed line. They commanded all the ground behind, as well as in front of them, and together constituted a favorable position for *the enemy* to hold. This was one good reason for our taking possession of it. It would, it is true, in our hands present a salient angle, which generally exposes both its sides to enfilade fires; but here the ridges were so high that each would serve as a "traverse" for the other, and reduce that evil to a minimum. On the other hand it would so greatly lengthen our line — which in any case must rest on Round Top, and connect with the left of the Second Corps — as to require a larger force than the Third Corps alone to hold it, and it would be difficult to occupy to the front of the "direct line" than it appeared from the orchard itself. In fact there was a third line between them, which appears, as seen from the orchard, to be continuous with Cemetery Ridge, but is nearly six hundred yards in front of it. This is the open ground east of Plum Run already described, and which may be called the Plum Run line. Its left where it crosses the run abuts rather on Devil's Den than Round Top; it was commanded by the much higher Peach Orchard crests, and therefore not an eligible line to occupy, although it became of importance during the battle.

As to the other two lines, the choice between them would depend on circumstances. The direct short line through the woods,

THE DEAD IN THE "WHEAT-FIELD," GATHERED FOR BURIAL. (FROM PHOTOGRAPHS.) 18

and strengthen the angle if the enemy already held the wood in its front. At my instance General Sickles ordered a couple of companies to ascertain if the wood was occupied.

About this time a cannonade was opened at Cemetery Hill, which indicated an attack there, and as I had examined the Emmettsburg Ridge, I said I would not wait the result of the reconnoissance, but return to headquarters by way of Round Top, and examine that part of the proposed line. As I was leaving, General Sickles asked me if he should move forward his corps. I answered, "Not on my authority; I will report to General Meade for his instructions." I had not reached the Wheat-field when a sharp rattle of musketry showed that the enemy held the wood in front of the Peach Orchard angle.

As I rode back, a view from that direction showed how much farther Peach Orchard was and including the Round Tops, could be occupied, intrenched, and made impregnable to a front attack. But, like that of Culp's Hill, it would be a purely defensive one, from which, owing to the nature of the ground and the enemy's commanding position on the ridges at the angle, an advance in force would be impracticable. The salient line proposed by General Sickles, although much longer, afforded excellent positions for our artillery; its occupation would cramp the movements of the enemy, bring us nearer his lines, and afford us facilities for taking the offensive. It was in my judgment the better line of the two, provided it were strongly occupied, for it was the only one on the field from which we could have passed from the defensive to the offensive with a prospect of decisive results. But General Meade had not, until the arrival of the Sixth Corps, a sufficient number of troops at his disposal to risk such an extension of his lines; it would have required both the Third and Fifth Corps, and left him without any reserve. Had he known that Lee's attack would be postponed until four P. M., he might have occupied this line in the morning; but he did not know this, expected an attack at any moment, and in view of the vast interests involved, adopted a defensive policy, and ordered the occupation of the *safe* line. In taking risks, it would not be for his army alone, but also for Philadelphia, Baltimore, and Washington, with the political consequences of their capture. Gettysburg was not a good strategical position for us, and the circumstances under which our army was assembled limited us tactically to a strictly defensive battle.

After finishing my examination I returned to headquarters and briefly reported to General Meade that the proposed line was a good one in itself, that it offered favorable positions for artillery, but that its relations to other lines were such that I could not advise, and suggested that he examine it himself before ordering its occupation. He nodded assent, and I proceeded to Cemetery Hill.

The cannonade there still continued; it had been commenced by the enemy, and was accompanied by some movements of troops towards our right. As soon as I saw that it would lead to nothing serious, I returned direct to the Peach Orchard, knowing that its occupation would require large reënforcements of artillery. I was here met by Captain Randolph, the corps chief of artillery,[19] who informed me that he had been ordered to place his batteries on the new line. Seeing Generals Meade and Sickles, not far off, in conversation, and supposing that General Meade had consented

BRIGADIER-GENERAL SAMUEL K. ZOOK, COMMANDING THE THIRD BRIGADE OF CALDWELL'S DIVISION, KILLED IN THE "WHEATFIELD" JULY 2D. (FROM A PHOTOGRAPH BY BRADY.)

to the occupation, I sent at once to the reserve for more artillery, and authorized other general officers to draw on the same source. Here perhaps I may be allowed to say *en passant* that this large reserve, organized by the wise forethought of General McClellan, sometimes threatened with destruction, and once actually broken up, was often, as at Malvern Hill, and now at Gettysburg, an invaluable resource in the time of greatest need. When in 1864 in the Rapidan campaign it was "got rid of," it reconstituted itself, without orders, and in a few weeks, through the necessities of the army, showing that "principles vindicate themselves."

When I arrived Birney's division was already posted on the crest from Devil's Den to the Peach Orchard, and along the Emmettsburg road, Ward's brigade on the left, Graham's at the angle, De Trobriand's connecting them by a thin line. Humphreys's division was on Graham's right, near the Emmettsburg road, Carr's brigade in the front line, about the Smith house,[20] Brewster's in second line. Burling's, with the exception of Sewell's Fifth New Jersey Regiment, then in skirmish order at the front, was sent to reënforce Birney. Seeley's battery, at first posted on the right, was soon after sent to the left of the Smith house, and replaced on the right by Turnbull's from the Artillery Reserve. Randolph had ordered Smith's battery, Fourth New York, to the rocky hill at the Devil's Den; Winslow's to the Wheat-field. He had placed Clark on the crest looking south, and his own ("E," First Rhode Island) near the angle, facing west. The whole corps was, however, too weak for the ground to be covered, and it was too late for Meade to withdraw it. Sykes's Fifth Corps had already been ordered up and was

COLONEL GEORGE L. WILLARD, COMMANDING THE THIRD BRIGADE OF HAYS'S DIVISION, KILLED ON JULY 2D. (FROM A PHOTOGRAPH BY BRADY.)

INSIDE EVERGREEN CEMETERY, CEMETERY HILL.
(BY EDWIN FORBES, AFTER HIS SKETCH MADE AT THE TIME.)

momentarily expected. As soon as fire opened, which was just as he arrived on the ground, General Meade sent also for Caldwell's division from Cemetery Ridge, and a division of the Twelfth Corps from Culp's, and soon after for troops from the Sixth Corps. McGilvery's artillery brigade soon arrived, from the reserve, and Bigelow's, Phillips's, Hart's, Ames's, and Thompson's batteries had been ordered into position on the crests, when the enemy opened from a long line of guns, stretching down to the crossing of the Emmettsburg pike. Smith's position at Devil's Den gave him a favorable oblique fire on a part of this line, and as he did not reply, I proceeded to the Den. Finding the acclivity steep and rocky, I dismounted and tied my horse to a tree before crossing the valley. My rank, brigadier-general, the command being that of a lieutenant-general, gave me a very small and insufficient staff, and even this had been recently cut down. The inspector of artillery Lieutenant-Colonel Warner, adjutant-general Captain Craig, my only aide Lieutenant Bissel, my one orderly, and even the flag-bearer necessary to indicate my presence to those seeking me, were busy conveying orders or messages, and I was alone; a not infrequent and an awkward thing for a general who had to keep up communications with every part of a battle-field and with the general-in-chief. On climbing to the summit, I found that Smith had just got his guns, one by one, over the rocks and chasms, into an excellent position. After pointing out to me the advancing lines of the enemy, he opened, and very effectively. Many guns were immediately turned on him, relieving so far the rest of the line. Telling him he would probably lose his battery, I left to seek for infantry supports, very doubtful if I would find my horse, for the storm of shell bursting over the place was enough to drive any animal wild. On reaching the foot of the cliff, I found myself in a plight at once ludicrous, painful, and dangerous. A herd of horned cattle had been driven into the valley between Devil's Den and Round Top, from which they could not escape. A shell had exploded in the body of one of them, tearing it to pieces; others were torn and wounded. All were *stampeded*, bellowing and rushing in their terror first to one side, then to the other, to escape the shells that were bursting over and amongst them.[21] Cross I must, and in doing so I had my most trying experience of the battle of Gettysburg. Luckily the poor beasts were as much frightened as I was, but their rage was subdued by terror, and they were good enough to let me pass through scot-free, but "badly demoralized." However, my horse was safe, I mounted, and in the busy excitement that followed almost forgot my scare.

It was not until about four P. M. that Longstreet got his two divisions into position in two lines, McLaws's on the right of Anderson's division of Hill's corps, and opposite the Peach Orchard; Hood's on the extreme Confederate right and crossing the Emmettsburg road. Hood had been ordered, keeping his left on that road, to break in the end of our line, supposed to be at the orchard; but perceiving that our left was "refused" (bent back towards Devil's Den), and noticing the importance of Round Top, he suggested to Longstreet that the latter be turned and attacked. The reply was that General Lee's orders were to attack along the Emmettsburg road. Again Hood sent his message and received the same reply, notwithstanding which he directed Law's brigade upon Round Top, in which movement a portion of Robertson's brigade joined, and the rest of the division was thrown upon Devil's Den and the ridge between it and the Peach Orchard. The first assaults were repulsed, but, after hard fighting, McLaws's division

THE SECOND DAY AT GETTYSBURG.

COLONEL EDWARD E. CROSS, COMMANDING THE FIRST BRIGADE OF CALDWELL'S DIVISION, KILLED NEAR DEVIL'S DEN, JULY 2D. (FROM A PHOTOGRAPH BY BRADY.)

being also advanced, the angle was, towards six o'clock, broken in, after a resolute defense and with great loss on both sides. In the mean time three of Anderson's brigades were advancing on Humphreys, and the latter received orders from Birney, now in command of the corps, Sickles being severely wounded soon after six o'clock near the Trostle house, to throw back his left, form an oblique line in his rear, and connect with the right of Birney's division, then retiring. The junction was not effected, and Humphreys, greatly outnumbered, slowly and skillfully fell back to Cemetery Ridge, Gibbon sending two regiments and Brown's Rhode Island battery to his support. But the enemy was strong and covered the whole Second Corps front, now greatly weakened by detachments. Wilcox's, Perry's, and Wright's brigades pressed up to the ridge, outflanking Humphreys's right and left, and Wright broke through our line and seized the guns in his front, but was soon driven out, and not being supported all fell back, about dusk, under a heavy artillery fire.

As soon as Longstreet's attack commenced, General Warren was sent by General Meade to see to Little Round Top. He found it unoccupied by troops, and seeing the advance of Hood's lines, and also the near approach of Sykes's Fifth Corps from Rock Creek, immediately caused Weed's and Vincent's brigades and Hazlett's battery to be detached from the latter and hurried them to the summit. The passage of the six guns through the roadless woods and amongst the rocks was marvelous. Under ordinary circumstances it would have been considered an impossible feat, but the eagerness of the men to get into action with their comrades of the infantry, and the skillful driving, brought them without delay to the very summit, where they went immediately into battle. They were barely in time, for the enemy were also climbing the hill. A close and bloody hand-to-hand struggle ensued, which

CONFEDERATE PRISONERS ON THE BALTIMORE PIKE. (BY EDWIN FORBES, AFTER HIS SKETCH MADE AT THE TIME.)

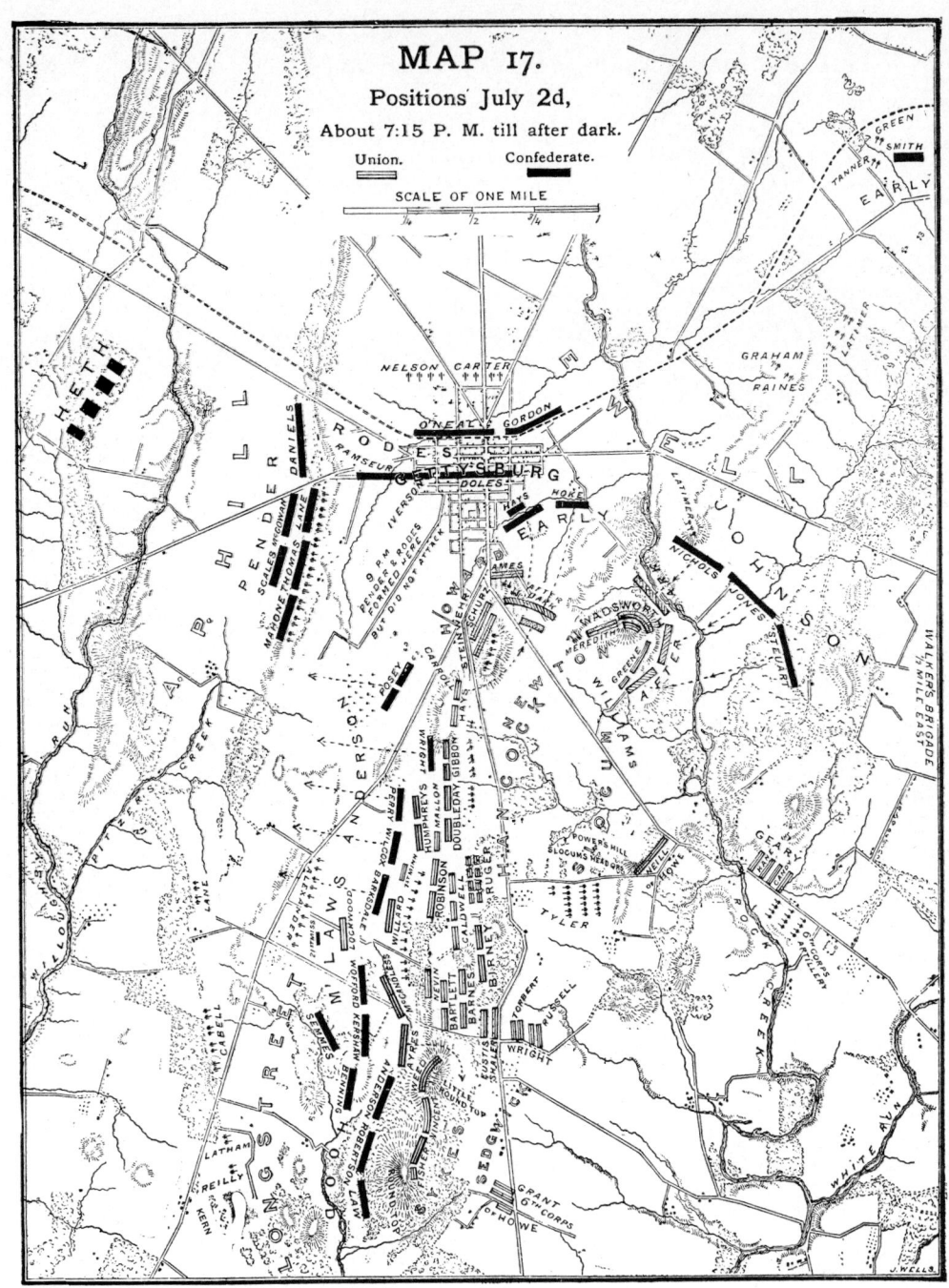

left both Round Tops in our possession. Weed and Hazlett were killed, and Vincent mortally wounded—all young men of great promise. Weed had served with much distinction as an artillerist in the Peninsular, Second Bull Run, and Antietam campaigns, had become chief of artillery of his army corps, and at Chancellorsville showed such special aptitude and fitness for large artillery commands that he was immediately promoted from captain to brigadier-general and transferred to the infantry. Hazlett was killed whilst bending over his former chief, to receive his last message, and Lieutenant Rittenhouse efficiently commanded the battery during the remainder of the battle.

The enemy, however, clung to the woods and rocks at the base of Round Top, carried Devil's Den and its woods, and captured three of Smith's guns, who, however, effectively deprived the enemy of their use by carrying off all the implements.[22]

The breaking in of the Peach Orchard angle exposed the flanks of the batteries on its crests, which retired firing, in order to cover the retreat of the infantry. Many guns of different batteries had to be abandoned because of the destruction of their horses and men; many were hauled off by hand; all the batteries lost heavily. Bigelow's Ninth Massachusetts made a stand close by the Trostle house in the corner of the field through which he had retired fighting with prolonges fixed. Although already much cut up, he was directed by McGilvery to hold that point at all hazards until a line of artillery could be formed in front of the wood beyond Plum Run; that is, on what we have called the "Plum Run line." This line was formed by collecting the serviceable batteries, and fragments of batteries, that were brought off, with which, and Dow's Maine battery fresh from the reserve, the pursuit was checked. Finally some twenty-five guns formed a solid mass,[23] which unsupported by infantry held this part of the line, aided Humphreys's movements, and covered by its fire the abandoned guns on the field until they could be brought off, as all were, except perhaps one.[24] When, after fully accomplishing its purpose, all that was left of Bigelow's battery was withdrawn, it was closely pressed by Humphries's Twenty-first Mississippi, the only Confederate regiment which succeeded in crossing the run. His men had entered the battery and fought hand-to-hand with the cannoneers; one was killed whilst trying to spike a gun, and another knocked down with a handspike whilst endeavoring to drag off a prisoner. Of the four battery-officers

CONFEDERATE SKIRMISHERS AT THE FOOT OF CULP'S HILL.

one was killed, another mortally, and a third, Captain Bigelow, severely wounded. Of seven sergeants, two were killed and four wounded; or a total of twenty-eight men, including two missing; and eighty out of eighty-eight horses were killed and wounded. As the battery had sacrificed itself for the safety of the line, its work is specially noticed as typical of the service that artillery is not infrequently called upon to render, and did render in other instances at Gettysburg besides this one.

When Sickles was wounded General Meade directed Hancock to take command of the Third as well as his own corps, which he again turned over to Gibbon. About 7:15 P. M., the field was in a critical condition. Birney's division was now broken up; Humphreys's was slowly falling back, under cover of McGilvery's guns; Anderson's line was advancing. On its right, Barksdale's brigade, except the Twenty-first Mississippi, was held in check only by McGilvery's artillery, to whose support Hancock now brought up Willard's brigade, of the Second Corps. Placing the Thirty-ninth New York in reserve,[25] Willard with his other three regiments charged Barksdale's brigade and drove

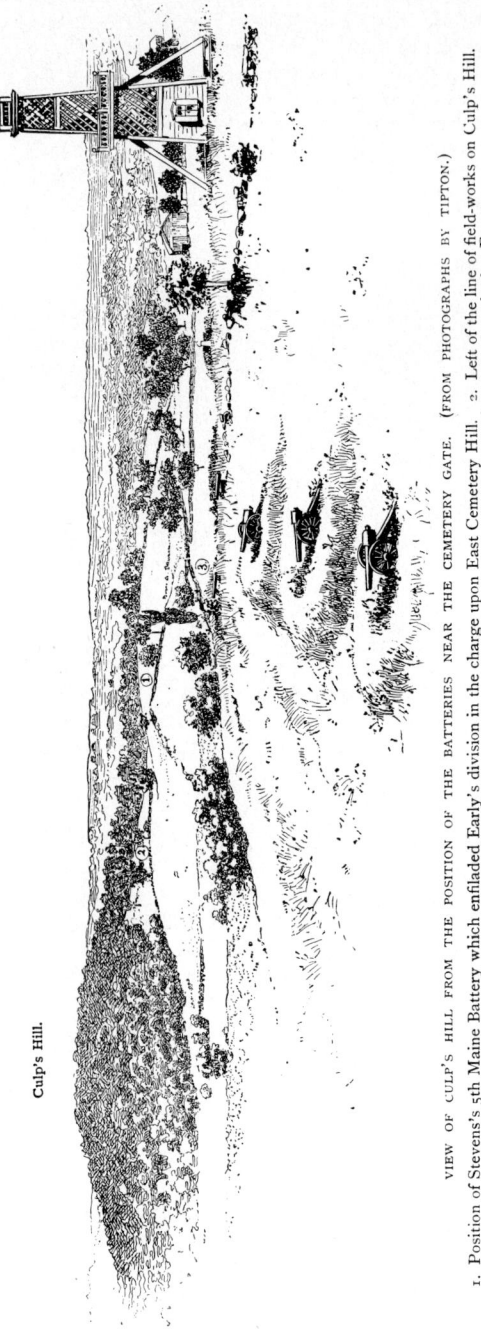

VIEW OF CULP'S HILL FROM THE POSITION OF THE BATTERIES NEAR THE CEMETERY GATE. (FROM PHOTOGRAPHS BY TIPTON.)

1. Position of Stevens's 5th Maine Battery which enfiladed Early's division in the charge upon East Cemetery Hill. 2. Left of the line of field-works on Culp's Hill. 3. Position of the 33d Massachusetts behind the fence of a lane where the left of the Confederate charge was repulsed.—EDITOR.

the men of Watson's battery ("I," Fifth United States), on the extreme left of McGilvery's line, but was in turn driven off by the Thirty-ninth New York led by Lieutenant Peeples of the battery, musket in hand, who thus recovered his guns, Watson being severely wounded.

Birney's division once broken, it was difficult to stem the tide of defeat. Hood's and McLaws's divisions—excepting Barksdale's brigade—compassed the Devil's Den and its woods, and as the Federal reënforcements from other corps came piecemeal, they were beaten in detail until by successive accretions they greatly outnumbered their opponents, who had all the advantages of position, when the latter in turn retired, but were not pursued. This fighting was confined almost wholly to the woods and Wheat-field between the Peach Orchard and Little Round Top, and the great number of brigade and regimental commanders, as well as of inferior officers and soldiers, killed and wounded on both sides, bears testimony to its close and desperate character. General Meade was on the ground active in bringing up and putting in reënforcements, and in doing so had his horse shot under him. At the close of the day the Confederates held the base of the Round Tops, Devil's Den, its woods, and the Emmettsburg road, with skirmishers thrown out as far as the Trostle house[26]; the Federals had the two Round Tops, the Plum Run line, and Cemetery Ridge. During the night the Plum Run line, except the wood on its left front (occupied by McCandless's brigade, Crawford's division, his other brigade being on Big Round Top), was abandoned; the Third Corps was massed to the left and rear of Caldwell's division, which had reoccupied its short ridge, with McGilvery's artillery on its crest. The Fifth Corps remained on and about Round Top, and Ruger's division of the Twelfth returned to Culp's Hill.

When Longstreet's guns were heard, Ewell opened a cannonade, which after an hour's firing was overpowered by the Federal artillery on Cemetery Hill. Johnson's division then advanced, and found only one brigade—Greene's—of the Twelfth Corps in position, the others having been sent to the aid of Sickles at the Peach Orchard. Greene fought with skill and determination for two or three hours, and, reënforced by seven or eight hundred men of the First and Eleventh Corps, succeeded in holding his own intrenchments, the enemy taking possession of the abandoned works of Geary and Ruger. This brought Johnson's troops near the Baltimore pike, but the darkness prevented their seeing or profiting by the advantage then within their reach. When Ruger's division returned from Round Top, and Geary's from Rock Creek,

it back nearly to the Emmettsburg road, when he was himself repulsed by a heavy artillery and infantry fire, and fell back to his former position near the sources of Plum Run. In this affair Willard was killed and Barksdale mortally wounded. Meanwhile the Twenty-first Mississippi crossed the run from the neighborhood of the Trostle house, and drove out

BRIGADIER-GENERAL STEPHEN H. WEED, COMMANDING THE THIRD BRIGADE OF AYRES'S DIVISION, KILLED JULY 2D. (FROM A PHOTOGRAPH BY BRADY.)

General Weed was picked off by sharpshooters in Devil's Den soon after getting his brigade in position on Little Round Top.—EDITOR.

they found Johnson in possession of their intrenchments, and immediately prepared to drive him out at daylight.

It had been ordered that when Johnson engaged Culp's Hill, Early and Rodes should assault Cemetery Hill. Early's attack was made with great spirit, by Hoke's and Avery's brigades, Gordon's being in reserve; the hill was ascended through the wide ravine between Cemetery and Culp's hills, a line of infantry on the slopes was broken, and Wiederich's Eleventh Corps, and Ricketts's reserve batteries near the brow of the hill overrun; but the excellent position of Stevens's twelve-pounders at the head of the ravine, which enabled him to sweep it, the arrival of Carroll's brigade sent unasked by Hancock,— a happy inspiration, as this line had been weakened to send supports both to Greene and Sickles,— and the failure of Rodes to coöperate with

DEVIL'S DEN, FACING LITTLE ROUND TOP.

EARLY'S CHARGE ON THE EVENING OF JULY 2D UPON EAST CEMETERY HILL.

Early, caused the attack to miscarry. The cannoneers of the two batteries so summarily ousted rallied, and recovered their guns by a vigorous attack with pistols by those who had them, by others with handspikes, rammers, stones, and even fence-rails; the "Dutchmen" showing that they were in no way inferior to their "Yankee" comrades, who had been "running" them ever since Chancellorsville. After an hour's desperate fighting the two Confederate brigades were driven out with heavy loss, Avery being among the killed.

At the close of this second day a consultation of corps commanders was held at General Meade's headquarters. I was not present, although summoned, but was informed that the vote was unanimous to hold our lines, and to await an attack for at least one day before taking the offensive, and General Meade so decided.

HAND-TO-HAND FOR RICKETTS'S GUNS.

GROUND OVER WHICH PICKETT CHARGED, AS SEEN FROM THE UNION LINES. (FROM A PHOTOGRAPH BY TIPTON.)
On the left is seen the clump of trees which was the point of direction for Pickett's men; also the monument of Webb's brigade near which General Webb was wounded. General Armistead was killed in the middle foreground of the picture; Codori's house is seen on the right.— EDITOR.

THE THIRD DAY AT GETTYSBURG.

A PENNSYLVANIA BUCKTAIL.

IN view of the successes gained on the second day, General Lee resolved to renew his efforts. These successes were:

1st. *On the right*, the lodgment at the base of the Round Tops, the possession of Devil's Den and its woods,[27] and the ridges on the Emmettsburg road which gave him the coveted positions for his artillery.

2d. *On the left*, the occupation of part of the intrenchments of the Twelfth Corps with an outlet to the Baltimore pike, by which all our lines could be taken in reverse.

3d. *At the center*, the partial success of three of Anderson's brigades in penetrating our lines, from which they were expelled only for lack of proper support.[28]

It was thought that better concert of action might have made good a lodgment here also.[29] Both armies had indeed lost heavily, but the account in that respect seemed in favor of the Confederates, or at worst balanced. Pickett's and Johnson's divisions[30] were fresh, as were Posey's and Mahone's brigades of Anderson's, and Smith's brigade of Early's division. These could be depended upon for an assault; the others could be used as supports, and to follow up a success. The artillery was almost intact.[31] Stuart had rejoined with his cavalry, excepting the brigades of Jones and Robertson, guarding the communications; and Imboden had also come up. General Lee, therefore, directed the renewal of operations both on the right and left. Ewell had been ordered to attack at daylight on July 3d, and during the night reënforced Johnson with Smith's, Daniel's, and O'Neal's brigades. Johnson had made his preparations, and was about moving, when at dawn Williams's artillery opened upon him, preparatory to an assault by Geary and Ruger for the recovery of their works. The suspension of this fire was followed by an immediate advance by both sides. A conflict ensued which lasted with varying success until near eleven o'clock, during which the Confederates were driven out of the Union intrenchments by Geary and Ruger, aided by Shaler's brigade of the Sixth Corps. They made one or two attempts to regain possession, but were unsuccessful, and a demonstration to turn Johnson's left caused him to withdraw his command to Rock Creek. The scene of this conflict was, at the close of the war, covered by a forest of dead trees, leaden bullets proving as fatal to them as to the soldiers whose bodies were thickly strewn beneath them.

Longstreet's arrangements had been made to re-attack Round Top, and his orders issued with a view to turning it, when General Lee decided that the assault should be made on Cemetery Ridge by Pickett's and Pettigrew's divisions, with part of Trimble's. Longstreet formed these in two lines — Pickett on the right, supported by Wilcox; Pettigrew on the left, with Lane's and Scales's brigades under Trimble in the second line. Hill was ordered to hold his line with the remainder of his corps, — six brigades, — give Longstreet assistance if required, and avail himself of any success that might be gained. Finally a powerful artillery force, about one hundred and fifty guns, was ordered to prepare the way for the assault by a cannonade.[32] The necessary arrangements caused delay, and before notice of this could be received by Ewell, Johnson, as we have seen, was attacked, so that the contest was over on the left before that at the center was begun. The hoped-for concert of action in the Confederate attacks was lost from the beginning.

On the Federal side Hancock's corps held Cemetery Ridge with Robinson's division, First Corps, on Hays's right in support, and Doubleday's at the angle between Gibbon and Caldwell. General Newton, having been assigned to the command of the First Corps, *vice* Reynolds, was now in charge of the ridge held by Caldwell. Compactly arranged on its crest was McGilvery's artillery, forty-one guns,[33] consisting of his own batteries, reënforced by others from the Artillery Reserve. Well to the right, in front of Hays and Gibbon, was the artillery of the Second Corps under its chief, Captain Hazard. Woodruff's battery was in front of Ziegler's Grove; on his left, in succession, Arnold's Rhode Island, Cushing's United States, Brown's Rhode Island, and Rorty's New York. In the fight of the preceding day the two last-named batteries had been to the front and suffered severely. Lieutenant T. Fred Brown was severely wounded, and his command devolved on Lieutenant Perrin. So great had been the loss in men and horses that they were now of four guns each, reducing the total number in the corps to twenty-six. Daniels's battery of horse artillery, four guns, was between Hazard and McGilvery at the angle.[34] In addition, some of the guns on Cemetery Hill, and Rittenhouse's on Little Round Top, could be brought to bear, but these were offset by batteries similarly placed on the flanks of the enemy, so that on the Second Corps line, within the space of a mile, were seventy-one guns[35] to oppose nearly one hundred and fifty.[36] They were on an open crest plainly visible from all parts of the opposite line. Between ten and eleven A. M., everything looking favorable at Culp's Hill, I crossed over to Cemetery Ridge, to see what might be going on at other points. Here a magnificent display greeted my eyes. Our whole

STEUART'S BRIGADE RENEWING THE CONFEDERATE ATTACK ON CULP'S HILL, MORNING OF THE THIRD DAY.

THE THIRD DAY AT GETTYSBURG.

MONUMENT OF THE SECOND MASSACHUSETTS INFANTRY, FACING THE EAST BASE OF CULP'S HILL.

front for two miles was covered by batteries already in line or going into position. They stretched—apparently in one unbroken mass—from opposite the town to the Peach Orchard, which bounded the view to the left, the ridges of which were planted thick with cannon. Never before had such a sight been witnessed on this continent, and rarely, if ever, abroad. What did it mean? It might possibly be to hold that line whilst its infantry was sent to aid Ewell, or to guard against a counter-stroke from us, but it most probably meant an assault on our center, to be preceded by a cannonade in order to crush our batteries and shake our infantry; at least to cause us to exhaust our ammunition in reply, so that the assaulting troops might pass in good condition over the half mile of open ground which was beyond our effective musketry fire. With such an object the cannonade would be long and followed immediately by the assault, their whole army being held in readiness to follow up a success. From the great extent of ground occupied by the enemy's batteries, it was evident that all the artillery on our west front, whether of the army corps or the reserve, must concur as a *unit*, under the chief of artillery, in the defense. This is provided for in all well-organized armies by special rules, which formerly were contained in our own army regulations, but they had been condensed in successive editions into a few short lines, so obscure as to be practically worthless, because, like the rudimentary toe of the dog's paw, they had become, from lack of use, mere survivals; unintelligible except to the specialist. It was of the first importance to subject the enemy's infantry, from the first moment of their advance, to such a cross-fire of our artillery as would break their formation, check their impulse, and drive them back, or at least bring them to our lines in such condition as to make them an easy prey. There was neither time nor necessity for reporting this

to General Meade, and beginning on the right, I instructed the chiefs of artillery and battery commanders to withhold their fire for fifteen or twenty minutes after the cannonade commenced, then to concentrate their fire with all possible accuracy on those batteries which were most destructive to us—but slowly, so that when the enemy's ammunition was exhausted, we should have sufficient left to meet the assault. I had just given these orders to the last battery on Little Round Top, when the signal gun was fired, and the enemy opened with all his guns. From that point the scene was indescribably grand. All their batteries were soon covered with smoke, through which the flashes were incessant, whilst the air seemed filled with shells, whose sharp explosions, with the hurtling of their fragments, formed a running accompaniment to the deep roar of the guns. Thence I rode to the Artillery Reserve to order fresh batteries and ammunition to be sent up to the ridge so soon as the cannonade ceased; but both the reserve and the train were gone to a safer place. Messengers, however, had been left to receive and convey orders, which I sent by them, and then returned to the ridge. Turning into the Taneytown pike, I saw evidence of the necessity under which the reserve had "decamped," in the remains of a dozen exploded caissons, which had been placed under cover of a hill, but which the shells had managed to search out. In fact, the fire was more dangerous behind the ridge than on its crest, which I soon reached at the position occupied by General Newton behind McGilvery's batteries, from which we had a fine view, as all our own guns were now in action.

Most of the enemy's projectiles passed over-

SLOCUM'S HEADQUARTERS, POWER'S HILL
[& the Nathaniel Lightner Farmhouse—KRG]

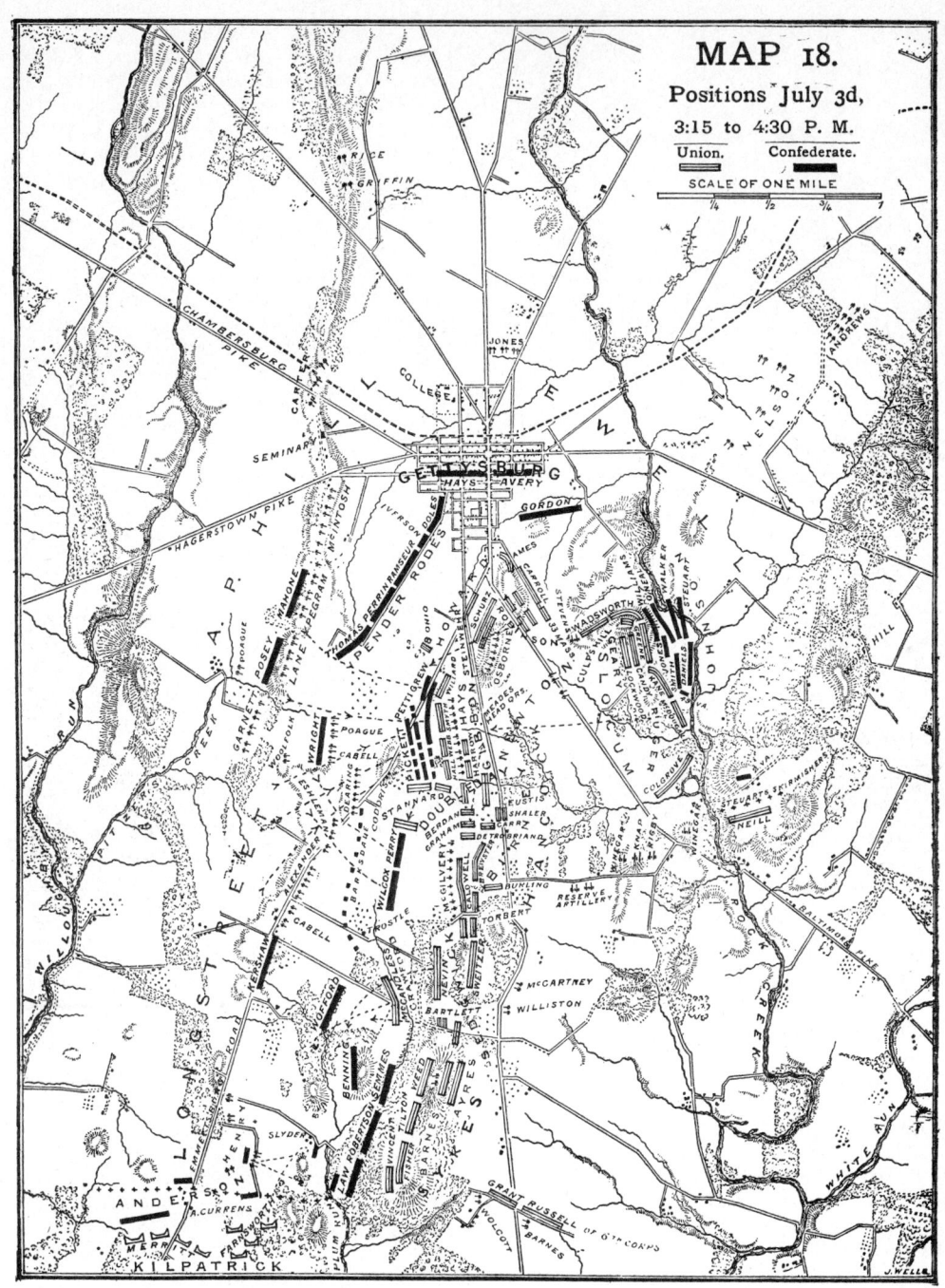

head, the effect being to sweep all the open ground in our rear, which was of little benefit to the Confederates — a mere waste of ammunition, for everything here could seek shelter. And just here an incident already published may be repeated, as it illustrates a peculiar feature of civil war. Colonel Long, who was at the time on General Lee's staff, had a few years before served in my mounted battery expressly to receive a course of instruction in the use of field artillery. At Appomattox we spent several hours together, and in the course of conversation I told him I was not satisfied with the conduct of this cannonade

PICKETT'S CHARGE, I.—THE UNION LINES BETWEEN THE "CLUMP OF TREES" AND THE ROUND TOPS.
(General Hancock and staff are seen in the left center of the picture.— This and the two pictures that follow are from the Cyclorama of Gettysburg, by permission of the National Panorama Company.)

which I had heard was under his direction, inasmuch as he had not done justice to his instruction; that his fire, instead of being concentrated on the point of attack, as it ought to have been, and as I expected it would be, was scattered over the whole field. He was amused at the criticism and said: "I remembered my lessons at the time, and when the fire became so scattered, wondered what you would think about it!"

I now rode along the ridge to inspect the batteries. The infantry were lying down on its reverse slope, near the crest, in open ranks, waiting events. As I passed along, a bolt from a rifle-gun struck the ground just in front of a man of the front rank, penetrated the surface and passed under him, throwing him "over and over." He fell behind the rear rank, apparently dead, and a ridge of earth where he had been lying reminded me of the backwoods practice of "barking" squirrels. Our fire was deliberate, but on inspecting the chests I found that the ammunition was running low, and hastened to General Meade to

![Pickett's Charge illustration]

"Clump of Trees."   Codori's.

PICKETT'S CHARGE, II.— THE MAIN COLLISION TO THE RIGHT OF THE "CLUMP OF TREES." (FROM THE CYCLORAMA OF GETTYSBURG.)
In this hand-to-hand conflict General Armistead was killed and General Webb was wounded.

advise its immediate cessation and preparation for the assault which would certainly follow. The headquarters building, immediately behind the ridge, had been abandoned, and many of the horses of the staff lay dead. Being told that the general had gone to the cemetery, I proceeded thither. He was not there, and on telling General Howard my object, he concurred in its propriety, and I rode back along the ridge, ordering the fire to cease. This was followed by a cessation of that of the enemy, under the mistaken impression that he had silenced our guns, and almost immediately his infantry came out of the woods and formed for the assault. On my way to the Taneytown road to meet the fresh batteries I had ordered up, I met Major Bingham, of Hancock's staff, who informed me that General Meade's aids were seeking me with orders to "cease firing"; so I had only anticipated his wishes. The batteries were found and brought up, and Fitzhugh's, Cowan's, and Parsons's put in near the clump of trees. Meantime the enemy advanced, and McGilvery opened an oblique destructive fire, reënforced by that of Rittenhouse's six rifle-guns from Round Top, which were served with remarkable accuracy, enfilading Pickett's lines. The Confederate approach was magnificent, and excited our admiration; but the story of that charge is so well known that I need not dwell upon it, further than concerns my own command. The steady fire from McGilvery and Rittenhouse, on their right, caused Pickett's men to "drift" in the opposite direction,[37] so that the weight of the assault fell upon the positions occupied by Hazard's batteries. I had counted

COLONEL ELIAKIM SHERRILL, COMMANDING THE THIRD BRIGADE OF HAYS'S DIVISION, SECOND CORPS, KILLED ON THE THIRD DAY.

THE THIRD DAY AT GETTYSBURG.

PICKETT'S CHARGE, III. — UNION TROOPS ADVANCING UPON PICKETT'S LEFT FLANK. (FROM THE GETTYSBURG CYCLORAMA.)

on an artillery cross-fire that would stop it before it reached our lines, but, except a few shots here and there, Hazard's batteries were silent until the enemy came within canister range. They had, unfortunately, exhausted their long-range projectiles during the cannonade, under the orders of their corps-commander,[38] and it was too late to replace them. Had my instructions been followed here, as they were by McGilvery, I do not believe that Pickett's division would have reached our line. We lost not only the fire of one-third of our guns, but the resulting cross-fire which would have doubled its value. The prime fault was in the obscurity of our army regulations as to the artillery, and the absence of all regulations as to the proper relations of the different arms of service to each other. On this occasion it cost us much blood, many lives, and for a moment endangered the success of the battle.[39] Soon after Pickett's repulse, Wilcox's, Wright's, and Perry's brigades were moved forward, but under the fire of the batteries in Gibbon's front and the fire of McGilvery's and Rittenhouse's guns, they soon fell back. The losses in the batteries of the Second Corps were very heavy. Rorty and Cushing were killed and Woodruff mortally wounded at their guns. So great was the destruction of men and horses, that Cushing's and Woodruff's United States and Brown's and Arnold's Rhode Island batteries were consolidated to form two serviceable ones.

The advance of the Confederate brigades to cover Pickett's retreat showed that the enemy's line opposite Cemetery Ridge was occupied by infantry, our own line on the ridge was in more or less disorder as the result of the conflict, and in no condition to advance a sufficient force for a counter assault. The largest bodies of organized troops available were on the left and General Meade now

BRIGADIER-GENERAL ELON J. FARNSWORTH, COMMANDING THE FIRST BRIGADE OF KILPATRICK'S CAVALRY DIVISION, KILLED ON THE THIRD DAY.

THE THIRD DAY AT GETTYSBURG.

GENERAL ALFRED PLEASONTON. GENERAL GEORGE A. CUSTER.
(FROM A PHOTOGRAPH TAKEN IN APRIL, 1863.)

THE THIRD DAY AT GETTYSBURG.

BRIGADIER-GENERAL CUSTER, COMMANDING THE SECOND BRIGADE OF KILPATRICK'S CAVALRY DIVISION AT GETTYSBURG.

MAJOR-GENERAL ALFRED PLEASONTON, COMMANDING THE CAVALRY CORPS AT GETTYSBURG.

proceeded to Round Top and pushed out skirmishers to feel the enemy in its front. An advance to the Plum Run line of the troops behind it would have brought them directly in front of the numerous batteries which crowned the Emmettsburg Ridge, commanding that line and all the intervening ground; a further advance, to the attack, would have brought them under additional heavy flank fires. McCandless's brigade, supported by Nevin's, was, however, pushed forward, under cover of the woods, which protected them from the fire of all these batteries; it crossed the Wheat-field, cleared the woods, and had an encounter with a portion of Benning's brigade, which was retiring. Hood's and McLaws's divisions were falling back under Longstreet's orders to their strong position, resting on Peach Orchard and covering Hill's line. It needs but a moment's examination of the official map to see that our troops on the left were locked up. As to the center, Pickett's and Pettigrew's assaulting divisions had formed no part of A. P. Hill's line, which was practically intact. The idea that there must have been "a gap of at least a mile" in that line, made by throwing forward these divisions, and that a prompt advance from Cemetery Ridge would have given us the line itself, or at least the artillery in front of it, was a delusion. A prompt counter-charge after a combat between two small bodies of men is one thing; the change from the defensive to the offensive of an army, after an engagement at a single point, is quite another. *This* was not a "Waterloo defeat" with a fresh army to follow it up, and to have made such a change to the offensive, on the assumption that Lee had made no provision against a reverse, would have been rash in the extreme. An advance of twenty thousand men from Cemetery Ridge in the face of the hundred and forty guns then in position would have been stark madness; an immediate advance from any point, in force, was simply impracticable, and before due preparation could have been made for a change to the offensive, the favorable moment — had any resulted from the repulse — would have passed away.

Whilst the main battle was raging, a sharp cavalry combat took place on our right between Stuart's command of four and Gregg's of three brigades; but Jenkins's Confederate brigade was soon thrown out of action from lack of ammunition, and two only of Gregg's were engaged. Stuart had been ordered to cover Ewell's left and was proceeding towards the Baltimore pike, where he hoped to create a diversion in aid of the Confederate infantry, and in case of Pickett's success to fall upon the retreating Federal troops. From near Cress's Ridge, two and a half miles east of Gettysburg, Stuart commanded a view of the roads

MONUMENT ON THE FIELD OF THE CAVALRY FIGHT BETWEEN THE FORCES OF GENERAL D. MCM. GREGG AND GENERAL J. E. B. STUART. (FROM A PHOTOGRAPH BY TIPTON.)

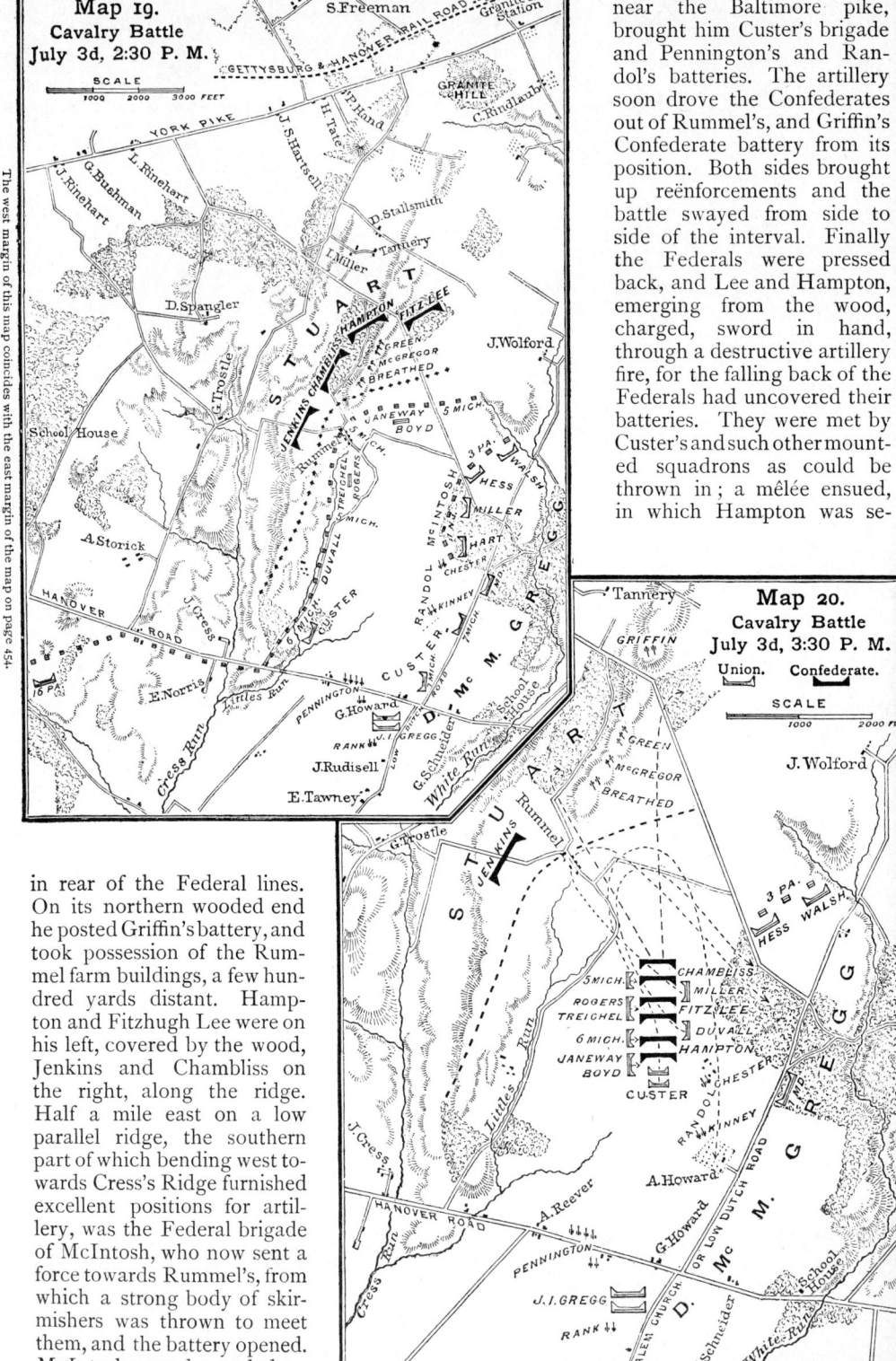

enforcements, and Gregg, then near the Baltimore pike, brought him Custer's brigade and Pennington's and Randol's batteries. The artillery soon drove the Confederates out of Rummel's, and Griffin's Confederate battery from its position. Both sides brought up reënforcements and the battle swayed from side to side of the interval. Finally the Federals were pressed back, and Lee and Hampton, emerging from the wood, charged, sword in hand, through a destructive artillery fire, for the falling back of the Federals had uncovered their batteries. They were met by Custer's and such other mounted squadrons as could be thrown in; a mêlée ensued, in which Hampton was se-

in rear of the Federal lines. On its northern wooded end he posted Griffin's battery, and took possession of the Rummel farm buildings, a few hundred yards distant. Hampton and Fitzhugh Lee were on his left, covered by the wood, Jenkins and Chambliss on the right, along the ridge. Half a mile east on a low parallel ridge, the southern part of which bending west towards Cress's Ridge furnished excellent positions for artillery, was the Federal brigade of McIntosh, who now sent a force towards Rummel's, from which a strong body of skirmishers was thrown to meet them, and the battery opened. McIntosh now demanded re-

THE THIRD DAY AT GETTYSBURG.

BATTLE BETWEEN THE UNION CAVALRY UNDER GREGG AND THE CONFEDERATE CAVALRY UNDER STUART.
(BY A. R. WAUD, AFTER HIS SKETCH MADE AT THE TIME.)

verely wounded and the charge repulsed. Breathed's and McGregor's Confederate batteries had replaced Griffin's, a sharp artillery duel took place, and at nightfall each side held substantially its original ground. Both sides claim to have held the Rummel house. The advantage was decidedly with the Federals, who had foiled Stuart's plans. Thus the battle of Gettysburg closed as it had opened, with a very creditable cavalry operation.

General Lee now abandoned the attempt to dislodge Meade; intrenched a line from Oak Hill to Peach Orchard; started all his *impedimenta* to the Potomac in advance, and followed with his army on the night of July 4, *via* Fairfield. This compelled Meade to take the circuitous routes through the lower passes; and the strategic advantage to Lee and disadvantage to Meade of Gettysburg, were made manifest.

General Meade has been accused of slowness in the pursuit. The charge is not well founded; he lost no time in commencing nor vigor in pushing it. On the morning of the 4th he ordered French at Frederick to seize and hold the lower passes, and put all the cavalry except Gregg's and McIntosh's brigades in motion to harass the enemy's anticipated retreat, and to destroy his trains and bridges at Williamsport. It stormed heavily that day, and the care of the wounded and burial of the dead proceeded, whilst the enemy's line was being reconnoitered. So soon, on the 5th, as it was certain that Lee was retreating, Gregg was started in pursuit on the Chambersburg pike, and the infantry — now reduced to a little over forty-seven thousand effectives, short of ammunition and supplies — by the lower passes. The Sixth Corps taking the Hagerstown road, Sedgwick reported the Fairfield pass fortified, a large force present, and that a fight could be had; upon which, on the 6th, Meade halted the rest of the infantry and ordered two corps to his support, but soon learning that although the pass could be carried it would cause too much delay, he resumed the march, leaving McIntosh and a brigade of the Sixth Corps to follow the enemy through the Fairfield pass. On the evening of the 4th Kilpatrick had a sharp encounter with the enemy in Monterey pass, and this was followed by daily cavalry combats on the different routes, in which much damage was done to trains and many captures of wagons, caissons, and prisoners effected. On the 5th French destroyed the pontoon bridge at Falling Waters. On the 6th Buford attacked at Williamsport and Kilpatrick toward Hagerstown, on his right, but as Imboden's train guard was strong, Stuart was up, and Longstreet close by, they had to withdraw. The enemy proceeded to construct a new bridge, and intrench a strong line covering Williamsport and Falling Waters. There were heavy rains on the 7th and 8th, but the infantry corps reached Middletown on the morning of the 9th, received supplies, crossed the mountains that day, and at its close the right was at Boonsboro', and the left at Rohrersville, on the roads to Hagerstown and Williamsport. The river was now greatly swollen

MAJOR-GENERAL GEORGE E. PICKETT. (FROM A PHOTOGRAPH BY COOK.)

and unfordable, and Halleck on the 10th advised Meade to postpone a general battle until his army was concentrated and his reënforcements up; but Meade, fully alive to the importance of striking Lee before he could cross the Potomac, advanced on that day and the 11th; and on the 12th pushed forward reconnoissances to feel the enemy. After a partial examination, made by himself and his chiefs of staff and of engineers, which showed that its flanks could not be turned, and that the line, so far as seen by them, presented no vulnerable points, he determined to make a demonstration in force on the next morning, the 13th, supported by the whole army, and to attack if a prospect of success offered. On assembling his corps-commanders, however, he found their opinion so adverse that he postponed it for further examination, after which he issued the order for the next day, the 14th. On advancing that morning, it was found that the enemy had abandoned his line and crossed the river, partly by fording, partly by a new bridge.

A careful survey of the enemy's intrenched line after it was abandoned justified the opinion of the corps-commanders against an attack, as it showed that an assault would have been disastrous to us. It proved also that Meade in overriding that opinion did not shrink from a great responsibility, notwithstanding his own recent experience at Gettysburg, where all the enemy's attacks on even partially intrenched lines had failed. If he erred on this occasion it was on the side of temerity.

But the hopes and expectations excited by the victory of Gettysburg were as unreasonable as the fears that had preceded it; and great was the disappointment that followed the "escape" of Lee's army. It was promptly manifested, too, and in a manner which indicates how harshly and unjustly the Army of the Potomac and its commanders were usually judged and treated; and what trials the latter had to undergo whilst subjected to the meddling and hectoring of a distant superior, himself but too often the mere mouthpiece of an irresponsible clique and from which they were not freed until the general-in-chief accompanied it in the field. That same day, before it was possible that all the circumstances could be known, three telegraphic despatches passed between the respective headquarters.

First. Halleck to Meade:

"I need hardly say to you that the escape of Lee's army without another battle has created great dissatisfaction in the mind of the President, and it will require an active and energetic pursuit on your part to remove the impression that it has not been sufficiently active heretofore."

Second. Meade to Halleck:

"Having performed my duty conscientiously and to the best of my ability, the censure of the President (conveyed in your dispatch of one P. M. this day) is in my judgment so undeserved, that I feel compelled most respectfully to ask to be immediately relieved from the command of this army."

Third. Halleck to Meade:

"July 14th my telegram stating the disappointment of the President at the escape of Lee's army was not intended as a censure, but as a stimulus to an active pursuit. It is not deemed a sufficient cause for your application to be relieved."

The losses of both armies were very large. The revised returns show for the Army of the Potomac: killed, 3063; wounded, 14,492; missing, 5435,— total, 22,990; and for the Army of Northern Virginia: killed, 2592; wounded, 12,706; missing, 5150,— total, 20,448. But the returns for the latter army are not complete; some commands are not reported, and in others the regimental show larger losses than do the brigade returns from which the foregoing numbers are compiled.

As to the comparative strength of the two armies on the field of battle, we have no satisfactory data. The last Confederate return was for May 31st, showing "Present for duty, under arms," 59,484, infantry. The morning report of the Army of the Potomac for June 30th shows "Present for duty, equipped," 77,208, infantry. Neither return is worth much except as a basis for guessing; the long marches, followed by the forced ones of July 1–2, of the Army of the Potomac, left thousands of stragglers on the roads. These totals are of little importance; they would have been of some significance had the larger army been defeated; but it was not. At the "points of contact" the Confederates were almost always the stronger. On July 1st, eighteen thousand Federal combatants contended against at least twenty-five thousand Confederates, and got the worst of it. On July 2d, Longstreet's fifteen thousand overcame Sickles's ten thousand, and had to halt when a larger force was opposed to them. Williams's Twelfth Corps retook its works from a larger body of Ewell's troops, as at the contested point they were opposed by an inferior number; and then held them, for Johnson's superior force was as much hampered here by the nature of the ground as was Meade's on the left, the evening before. In many respects the Confederates had the advantage: they had much better ground for their artillery; they were fresher; they were all veterans; they were better organized; they were commanded by officers selected for their experience and abilities, and in whom they had implicit confidence. These were enormous advantages, sufficient to counterbalance the difference of numbers; and whilst all the Confederate army, except here and there a brigade, were fought to the utmost, the strongest Federal corps (the Sixth) was hardly in action, the total loss of its eight brigades being but two hundred and forty-two killed, wounded, and missing. But the Southerners were subjected here to the disadvantages that the Northerners had to contend with in Virginia; they were surrounded by enemies, not friends who supplied them with aid and information; and they were not by choice, but necessity, the assailants on the chosen ground of their opponents.

Right gallantly did they act their part, and their failure carried no discredit with it. Their military honor was not tarnished by their defeat, nor their spirit lowered, but their respect for their opponents was restored to what it had been before Fredericksburg and Chancellorsville.

CONSECRATION OF THE GETTYSBURG CEMETERY, NOVEMBER 19TH, 1864—THE GATHERING THAT PRESIDENT LINCOLN ADDRESSED. (FROM A PHOTOGRAPH.)

CEMETERY RIDGE AFTER PICKETT'S CHARGE. (BY EDWIN FORBES, AFTER HIS SKETCH MADE AT THE TIME.)

The Question of Command on Cemetery Ridge:
a letter published in *Century Magazine* July 1887.

IN the March CENTURY Mrs. Warren publishes a letter of General Warren, written soon after the battle of Gettysburg, showing that General Meade's orders to him on the afternoon of July 2d were to look, not specifically to Round Top, as I have stated, but — a much wider mission — to the left of the army. I regret that I did not see that letter before writing my brief account, in which I dwelt less on General Warren's services than I would otherwise have done, because they were so universally recognized. The duty confided to him was a very responsible one, and, as the result shows, could not have been intrusted to better hands. The quickness with which he comprehended the threatened dangers in all their magnitude, when a simple incident revealed them to *him* as it would have done to few others, the apt measures he adopted to avert them, and, above all, the promptitude — his leading characteristic — with which he *acted*, saved both the Round Tops to us, disconcerted the enemy's plans, and proved General Warren to be what he was, one of the ablest and most meritorious of our generals.

In the same CENTURY General F. A. Walker of General Hancock's staff comments on my expressed belief that, had my instructions for the cannonade of July 3d been carried out by Captain Hazard, commander of the artillery of the Second Corps, the Confederate assault would not have reached our lines; and considers this "a very severe impeachment" of General Hancock's conduct of his artillery. I fully appreciate and honor the motive of General Walker's courteous criticism, and his very kind references to myself, but he writes under misapprehensions which are widespread and misleading, and which, as they place me in a false position, I beg leave to explain. He says:

"In the first place, two antagonistic theories of authority are advanced. General Hancock claimed that he commanded *the line of battle* along Cemetery Ridge. General Hunt in substance alleges that General Hancock commanded the infantry of that line, and that he himself commanded the artillery.

"Winfield S. Hancock did not read his commission as constituting him a major-general of infantry, nor did he believe that a line of battle was to be ordered by military specialists. He knew that by both law and reason the defense of Cemetery Ridge was intrusted to him, subject to the actual, authentic orders of the commander of the Army of the Potomac, but not subject to the discretion of one of General Meade's staff-officers. . .

"So much for the question of authority. On the question of policy there is only to be said that a difference of opinion appears . . . as to what was most expedient in a given emergency."

General Hancock's claim that he commanded all the troops of every description posted on his part of Cemetery Ridge is perfectly valid. It cannot be disputed, and I never questioned it. But all commands must be exercised subject to the established principles for the government of armies. Under these, commanders of special arms issue their own orders direct to their subordinates serving with army corps, who must submit them to the corps commanders with whom they serve. The latter, being supreme on their own lines, can modify or countermand these orders, but by doing so they make themselves responsible for the result. Thus all conflicts or theories as to authority are avoided. Our "Regulations" (Scott's), adopted in 1821, reads:

"The superior officer of the corps of engineers, or of the artillery, serving with one of the army corps . . . will receive the orders of the commandant thereof, to whom the said superior officer of engineers or of artillery will communicate any orders he may receive from his own particular commandant-in-chief, attached to general headquarters."

Separate paragraphs provided rules for the military "staff" and administration,— the latter including the supply departments. "Staff-officers" are forbidden to give orders except in the names of their generals. From this rule administrative officers are specially exempted, their chiefs directing their respective departments in their own names, but subject to the control of their generals, with whom they serve.

All these regulations are essential to the management of a large army, but are only partly applicable to a two-company post, the school in which most of our officers both of the war-office and of the regiments were trained. So in the "Regulations" of 1861-3, they were all condensed into one short paragraph:

"Staff officers, and commanders of artillery, engineers, and ordnance, report to their immediate commanders the state of the supplies and whatever concerns the service under their direction, and receive their orders; and communicate to them the orders they receive from their superiors in their own corps."

Closely examined, this is correct; but it is obscure and misleading. It lumps together officers of the staff and of administration as "staff-officers," and so connects them with those of the special arms as seemingly to confirm the erroneous idea that engineer officers are staff-officers and of course that artillery officers must be the same. It is an odd notion, which could not find a lodgment in any other army than our own, that an artillery commandant-in-chief, a "corps commander" himself to all intents and purposes, and provided with a staff of his own, is "one of the staff-officers" who runs about a battle-field carrying "the actual and authentic orders" of the general-in-chief to *other* corps commanders. A "staff-officer" is an officer below the rank of brigadier, attached to the person or headquarters of a general as his aide or assistant.

To illustrate the general principle as to the service of the special arms, I quote from the "Instructions of Frederick the Great" to his artillery. He was himself, by the way, an "artillery specialist" of the highest order, yet I have never heard it suggested that this unfitted him for "ordering a line of battle." He was also a disciplinarian of the sternest school, yet he "almost preached insubordination" in order to reduce to a minimum the mischief that meddling with the artillery by any general, even the general-in-chief, might occasion. He says:

"It sometimes happens that the general in command, or some other general, is himself forgetful, and orders the fire to be opened too soon, without considering what injurious consequences may result from it. In such case the artillery officer must certainly obey, but he should fire as slowly as possible, and point the pieces with the utmost accuracy, in order that his shots may not be thrown away."

As to the other question, that of policy, each general must decide it for himself, and General Hancock presumably acted according to his best judgment in the emergency suddenly presented to him when the cannonade opened. I do not know his reasons for countermanding my orders, and therefore cannot discuss them, even were I disposed to do so. As to the hypothetical case presented by General Walker, the possible effect of the enemy's cannonade on the *morale* of the troops, and his question, "Who was the better judge, General Hunt or General Hancock?" I may be permitted to reply, that a corps commander ought to be, so far as his own corps is concerned. It is, however, one of the necessary duties of an artillery commander to study the qualities of the other arms, for these must be considered in organizing and distributing the artillery, and are, as we see in this very case, important elements in determining its service. I had studied the Army of the Potomac, believed in its high qualities, and when, for special reasons, I instructed our batteries to withhold their fire for a given period, I knew the severity of the trial to which I was subjecting all the troops. I knew, also, that while the batteries would be the direct object of the enemy's fire, their men must stand idle at the guns and bear its full fury, while the infantry, lying on the reverse slope of the ridge and out of the enemy's sight, would be partly sheltered from it. Yet I felt no misgiving as to the fortitude of my cannoneers, and no doubt as to that of the infantry. I think I was justified by the event, for the troops on General Hancock's line where my instructions were not followed, and those on General Newton's line (on Hancock's immediate left), where they *were* followed, were in equal "heart and courage" for the "fearful ordeal of Longstreet's charge." The object of my orders, however, was to spare them this ordeal altogether by breaking up the charge before it reached our lines. Had my orders been fully carried out, I think their whole line would have been — as half of it was — driven back before reaching our position, and this would have given us our only chance for a successful counter-attack. As it was, the splendid valor of Pickett's division alone enabled the Confederates, although defeated, to preserve their *morale* intact.

Henry J. Hunt.

THE GETTYSBURG ADDRESS
*Delivered by Abraham Lincoln
to dedicate the
Gettysburg National Cemetery
November 19, 1863*

Four score and seven years ago our fathers brought forth on this continent a new nation, conceived in Liberty, and dedicated to the proposition that all men are created equal.

Now we are engaged in a great civil war, testing whether that nation, or any nation so conceived and so dedicated, can long endure. We are met on a great battlefield of that war. We have come to dedicate a portion of that field, as a final resting place for those who here gave their lives that that nation might live. It is altogether fitting and proper that we should do this.

But, in a larger sense, we cannot dedicate — we cannot consecrate — we cannot hallow — this ground. The brave men, living and dead, who struggled here, have consecrated it, far above our poor power to add or detract. The world will little note, nor long remember what we say here, but it can never forget what they did here. It is for us the living, rather, to be dedicated here to the unfinished work which they who fought here have thus far so nobly advanced. It is rather for us to be here dedicated to the great task remaining before us — that from these honored dead we take increased devotion to that cause for which they gave the last full measure of devotion — that we here highly resolve that these dead shall not have died in vain — that this nation, under God, shall have a new birth of freedom — and that government of the people, by the people, for the people, shall not perish from the earth.

FOOTNOTES ADDED TO TEXT
by Kathleen R. Georg, Research Historian,
National Park Service
Gettysburg National Military Park

[1] Lee's headquarters were in an orchard across the Chambersburg Pike from this "Thompson House", and therefore, behind the back of the photographer.

[2] This was the ideal situation, but it did not always hold true during the Gettysburg Campaign. Pegram's Battalion was composed of five batteries, while Alexander's old battalion had six batteries and Lane's Sumter Battalion had only three.

[3] Hunt is referring to the U.S. Regular (or standing) army artillery, and not to the numerous and fine volunteer organizations which were recruited as batteries throughout the northern states.

[4] Hunt probably was referring to campaign statistics. Regimental histories and official records do not bear out his figures for the Battle of Gettysburg. There were only 178 guns at the most with the Union infantry during the battle, 114 guns with the reserve artillery, and 44 guns at the most with the cavalry.

[5] These Union dead were not photographed on the First Day's field west of the seminary, but south of the town of Gettysburg, probably near the famous Peach Orchard on the Second Day's field.

[6] These dead soldiers were likewise photographed on the Second Day's field, south of Gettysburg.

[7] *Almost* through its entire length.

[8] These engravings from photographs taken shortly after the Battle of Gettysburg depict Confederate (not Union) dead near the Rose Woods (not the misnomered "McPherson Woods".). See William Frassanito's *Gettysburg: A Journey in Time* (New York: Charles Scribner's Sons, 1975) for a discussion of the oft-times misinterpreted Gettysburg photographs.

[9] Calif's two-gun section was just southeast of Reynolds Woods, called McPherson Woods by earlier historians (and perpetuated by later historians), but in reality owned by John Herst at the time of the battle and never owned by a McPherson. The McPherson Woods should be called the Herbst Woods.

[10] He was engaging more than double the number of his own guns. The Confederates had seventeen guns on Herr Ridge, while Calef had only six 3-inch rifled cannon.

[11] Without disparaging Hunt's obvious respect for John Reynolds, it is an over-estimation of the somewhat limited contributions of an officer who was on the field less than an hour before he was killed. He was struck by the Confederate ball before two infantry brigades were deployed to meet the enemy, and did little more than agree with Buford's estimation of the value of the ridgeline position. He proposed nothing new or startling (as far as tactics) which Buford had not already foreseen or taken care of. Reynolds did not live long enough to witness the valiant defense directed by Doubleday, but has somehow received credit from participants like Hunt for saving the day for the Union.

[12] That of Reynolds' Battery L, 1st New York Light Artillery.

[13] One Napoleon of Heckman's Battery K, 1st Ohio Light Artillery.

[14] Pender was not wounded until later in the afternoon of July 2.

[15] Hunt, responding to Slocum's fears that his line might be breached before his Twelfth Corps could make juncture with Wadsworth's Division on Culp's Hill, was determined to cover the rear of that hill, and thus the Baltimore Pike and the rear (inside) of the Federal "fish-hook" line. An astounding 47 guns from Osborn's, Muhlenberg's, and Fitzhugh's artillery brigades were placed along the Baltimore Pike from Evergreen Cemetery southward. Had Ewell's Confederate Corps broken through Slocum's line (as later-day critics think he could and should have done), it would have availed him nothing and he would have been pulverized by Hunt's concentrated pieces. Since this impressive number of cannon never fired a shot from their position, however, they have been oft-time ignored by students of the battle. They might have played a very valuable role in the salvation of the Union army had events gone differently.

[16] A fair and objective analysis by Hunt, who did not ever get along well with Meade personally.

[17] Many soldiers never learned that Meade was in command of the army at Gettysburg, and there were many others who had no confidence in Meade. Numerous incidents on the Second and Third Days of the Battle of Gettysburg recall the elation and confidence felt by the troops when rumors spread that McClellan was in command or on his way to the field of battle to assume command.

[18] This is not the wheatfield, but the field just west of Rose Woods. These are Confederate soldiers who belonged to Longstreet's Corps.

[19] Third Corps.

[20] Known at the time of the battle as the log Klingel farmhouse.

[21] Many farmers of the countryside had taken their horses and cattle to the Round Tops and Culp's Hill just before the battle in hopes of keeping them safe from the hands of both armies, which impressed the one animal into service and slaughtered the other beast for food.

[22] Smith's men denied the Confederates *immediate* use of the cannon, since they assumed they would be carried by a Union counterattack. Such did not occur, and Smith was humiliated to lose these three pieces. The Confederates brought them off the field, and used them to replace damaged cannon of the First Corps.

[23] There were never more than thirteen guns in this temporary Union back-up line (four of Rorty's, two of Thompson's, three of Phillips', and four of Dow's batteries).

[24] This was one of Thompson's rifled guns of Battery C & F, 1st Pennsylvania Light Artillery, which was eventually brought off by Confederates from between the lines early in the morning of July 3.

[25] Not a complete regiment at Gettysburg, the 39th New York infantry had only four companies present.

[26] The Confederates were not as far advanced as the Trostle farmhouse that night or else Dow's volunteers could not have recovered the guns abandoned by Bigelow just opposite the farmhouse.

[27] Devil's Den had no "woods", just a few scattered trees among the boulders. The woods referred to by Hunt were probably the Rose Woods and those at the base of Big Round Top.

[28] Hunt is mistaken in his statement that three brigades penetrated Union lines. Only Wright's Brigade briefly broke the Union infantry line just south of the Copse of Trees, momentarily capturing three of Weir's Napoleons. Perry and Wilcox did not advance beyond the brush-lined swale known as Codori Thicket, some 300 yards west of the main Union line along the ridge.

[29] The third-mentioned "success" by Wright's brigade may have been the over-riding reason why Lee chose his July 3rd tactics resulting in the frontal assault at the Copse of Trees (known as "Pickett's Charge"). If one brigade could break the center of the line momentarily, Lee reasoned that a much larger force, properly supported by artillery and reserve infantry, might successfully carry the position and win the battle.

[30] Johnson's Division of Ewell's Second Corps was not "fresh" in terms of not having seen action in the battle. On the evening of July 2, Johnson's Division (with the exception of Walker's Brigade) crossed Rock Creek and drove the enemy from the breastworks of Culp's Hill until darkness halted the attack.

[31] Confederate batteries, although none had been captured, had suffered as severely as Union cannon on July 1 and July 2, with probably more cannon damaged and equipped with unreliable and faulty ammunition than Hunt's guns by the end of July 2.

[32] Eventually, 152 Confederate cannon participated in the great cannonade.

[33] McGilvery commanded forty-nine guns belonging to the batteries of Daniels, Thomas, Thompson, Phillips, Hart, Sterling, Rank, Cooper, Dow, and Ames.

[34] Daniels' guns (supposedly six in number — four Parrots and two howitzers) were at the extreme right of McGilvery's line.

[35] The 28 guns of Hazard's Brigade brought the total of Union guns from Ziegler's Grove southward to the George Weikert lane to 77.

[36] Although Hunt refers to only the guns he had along his 1st and 2nd Corps front, he does not mention the other 45 Union cannon which participated in the cannonade from other points along the line. Altogether, 124 Union guns responded at one time or another to the Confederate 152 cannon. It appears that Hunt, like other Northern historians, exaggerated the numerical difference beyond its true proportions to give the Union artillery an "underdog" position, they therefore seem to swell the effectiveness of their fire.

[37] This "drifting" to their left by Pickett's Division was not so much caused by the firing of the Union batteries of McGilvery and Rittenhouse as by the necessity to oblique to the left (near the Codori buildings) in order to concentrate the attack on the famed Copse of Trees, the objective of the assaulting column.

[38] The commander referred to is Winfield S. Hancock, of the Union Second Corps; Hancock took personal responsibility for the whole of the line from the grove to Weikert's, and commanded a reluctant McGilvery to answer the Confederate fire during the cannonade against Hunt's orders. Incidentally, there were no Second Corps batteries in McGilvery's line.

[39] Hunt engaged in lengthy and bitter correspondence in his later years over this very point, believing that his military toes had been stepped on by Hancock's interference on July 3.